Capital Markets and Real Estate
How Money and Capital Shapes the Property Market

By Willem Tait

Published by WRT Publishing

Copyright © 2024 by Willem Tait
All rights reserved.

Copyright Warning:

No part of this publication may be reproduced, distributed, or transmitted in any form or by any means, including photocopying, recording, or other electronic or mechanical methods, without the prior written permission of the author, except in the case of brief quotations embodied in reviews and certain other noncommercial uses permitted by copyright law.

For permission requests, contact the author at:
willemtait@outlook.com

Disclaimer:

This eBook is for educational and informational purposes only. The author is not liable for any damages or losses arising from the use or misuse of the content in this book.

Cover Design: Time Brands
Published by WRT Publishing
First Edition

ISBN KDP Amazon Paperback: 9798302264121
ISBN KDP Amazon Hardcover: 9798302266545
ISBN Library Print: 978-0-6398578-0-0
ISBN Library eBook: 978-0-6398578-1-7

Why this Book?

Real estate is often considered the cornerstone of wealth creation. From family homes to sprawling commercial developments, it is an asset class that touches every aspect of life.

Yet, beyond its bricks and mortar lies a complex, interconnected world, the realm of capital markets. This book is your guide to understanding how these two dynamic forces converge to create opportunities, drive growth, and shape the global economy.

The truth is, most people don't realise how deeply capital markets influence the world of real estate. The homes we buy, the skyscrapers we admire, and even the funds we invest in are intricately linked to the flow of capital.

Whether you're a seasoned investor, an industry professional, or simply curious about how real estate and finance work together, this book will take you on a journey to demystify that connection.

The structure of this book is carefully designed to cater to readers of all backgrounds. The chapters ahead unravel the layers of complexity, starting with an introduction to capital markets and their role in real estate. We'll explore topics such as debt and equity financing, the rise of securitisation, and the growing influence of institutional investors.

Along the way, we'll examine how global trends, economic indicators, and innovative technologies are transforming both industries.

But this isn't just a book about technical concepts. It's a book about opportunities, your opportunities. My hope is to inspire you to see real estate and capital markets not as distant, impersonal systems but as accessible avenues for growth and prosperity.

By the end, you'll have a solid grasp of the key principles, tools, and strategies you need to navigate these markets confidently.

To get the most out of this book, I suggest reading it with a mindset of discovery. Each chapter builds on the last, but they're also designed to stand on their own, allowing you to dive into the topics that resonate most with you.

As you read, I encourage you to think critically and reflect on how these principles apply to your own life or work. Use the case studies and real-world examples as a lens to deepen your understanding. The concluding chapter will tie it all together, offering actionable strategies and a vision for the future of capital markets and real estate.

This book is the beginning of a conversation. It's a bridge between two powerful worlds, capital markets and real estate, and a guide to navigating the vast opportunities they offer.

So, whether you're a first-time investor, a seasoned professional, or just curious about the forces shaping our world, I invite you to turn the page and begin the journey.

Let's explore this intersection together.

Table of Contents

Why this Book?..2
Table of Contents 4
Introduction 11
Chapter 1: Capital Market vs. Real Estate 15
    The Tangible Meets the Financial......................17
    Investment as a Driving Force 18
    Strategy at the Core..19
    Challenges and Opportunities 20
    A Partnership for the Future 21
    Closing Thoughts..22
Chapter 2: The Foundation of Capital Markets........23
    Bonds and the Building Blocks of Capital 25
    Equities: Ownership and Opportunity 26
    Trading and Market Dynamics..........................28
    Liquidity: The Engine of Efficiency....................29
    Investors: The Lifeblood of Capital Markets 30
    Interlinking with Real Estate 32
    Conclusion: The Foundation for Growth 33
Chapter 3: Real Estate and Financial Ecosystems .34
    Diversification: Spreading Risk 38
    Real Estate's Role in the Financial Ecosystem 42
    Balancing Perspectives 43
    Conclusion: Real Estate as the Link 44
Chapter 4: Equity Financing for Real Estate............45
    Real Estate Investment Trusts (REITs):

    Democratizing Equity Investment 48
    Private Equity in Real Estate 50
    The Role of Equity in Portfolio Diversification ... 53
    Conclusion: The Power of Equity 55

Chapter 5: Debt Financing in Real Estate 56
    Bonds: Bridging Real Estate and Capital Markets
    60
    Debt Instruments: Beyond Mortgages and Bonds
    62
    Debt Financing's Link to Capital Markets 65
    Balancing Perspectives 66
    Conclusion: Building on Debt 67

Chapter 6: The Role of Institutional Capital 68
    Pension Funds: Long-Term Stability 71
    Insurance Companies: Balancing Risk and
    Returns 72
    Sovereign Wealth Funds: Global Reach 73
    Private Equity Funds: Strategic Partners 74
    Practical Examples: Institutional Capital in Action
    75
    Balancing Perspectives 77
    Conclusion: A Foundation for Growth 78

Chapter 7: Securitization and Real Estate 79
    What is Securitization? 81
    How Securitization Works 82
    The Role of Mortgage-Backed Securities (MBS)
    84
    Benefits of Securitization 86
    Practical Examples of Securitization 89

Building on Earlier Chapters 90
Looking Ahead 90
Conclusion: Unlocking Potential 91

Chapter 8: Private vs. Public Real Estate Market 92
Understanding Private Real Estate Markets 94
Public Real Estate Markets: Accessibility and Liquidity..96
Comparing Investment Strategies 98
Practical Examples 100
Balancing Perspectives 102
Looking Ahead 103
Conclusion: Two Markets, One Ecosystem 104

Chapter 9: Economic Indicators 105
GDP: The Pulse of Economic Health..............107
Inflation: The Silent Force 109
Interest Rates: The Cost of Capital.................111
The Interplay of Indicators 113
Practical Examples 114
Building on Previous Insights..........................115
Looking Ahead 116
Conclusion: Navigating Economic Forces 117

Chapter 10: Globalization of Real Estate 118
The Rise of Cross-Border Investments 120
Trends Driving Globalization...........................122
Challenges and Risks 124
Implications for Stakeholders..........................126
Practical Examples 127
Looking Ahead 128
Conclusion: A Borderless Future 129

Chapter 11: Risk Management 130
- Understanding Risk in Real Estate Capital Markets 131
- Common Risks in Real Estate Capital Markets 133
- Strategies for Risk Mitigation 135
- The Interplay of Risk and Opportunity 138
- Practical Examples 139
- Looking Ahead 140
- Conclusion: Navigating the Risks 141

Chapter 12: Alternative Investments 142
- The Nature of Alternatives in Real Estate 144
- Linked Markets and Strategic Diversification .. 147
- Structuring Alternative Investments: Lessons from Raising Money for Real Estate Investments 149
- Examples of Alternative Opportunities 151
- Risks and Considerations 153
- Looking Ahead 155
- Conclusion: Unlocking New Possibilities 156

Chapter 13: ESG and Sustainable Investing 157
- The Foundations of ESG 158
- The Rise of ESG in Real Estate 160
- Environmental Factors: Sustainability in Focus 162
- Social Factors: The Human Element 164
- Governance Factors: Accountability and Transparency 166
- Pros and Cons of ESG in Real Estate 168
- Effectiveness of ESG: Real-World Examples . 170

Looking Ahead 171
Conclusion: A Framework for the Future 172
Chapter 14: Future of Real Estate Markets 173
The Role of Technology in Real Estate Capital Markets 174
Blockchain: The Backbone of Transparent Transactions 176
    How Blockchain Works in Real Estate 176
    Use Cases of Blockchain in Real Estate ... 177
    Benefits of Blockchain 178
PropTech and Property Management 179
    Key Areas of PropTech 179
    The Impact of PropTech on Real Estate Capital Markets 180
Tokenization: The Future of Real Estate Investment 181
    How Tokenization Works 181
    Benefits of Tokenization 182
    Challenges of Tokenization 182
The Future of Real Estate Capital Markets 183
Conclusion: Embracing Innovation 184
Chapter 15: Case Studies 185
Case Study 1: Revitalizing Urban Cores ... 186
Case Study 2: Expanding Affordable Housing 187
Case Study 3: Logistics Hub Development 188
Case Study 4: Green Office Tower 189
Case Study 5: Cross-Border Retail Investment 190

    Case Study 6: Residential Tokenization ...191
    Case Study 7: Industrial Park Expansion..192
    Case Study 8: Healthcare Real Estate Fund 193
    Case Study 9: Student Housing Portfolio..194
    Case Study 10: Mixed-Use Urban Development...195
  Lessons from the Case Studies......................196
Chapter 16: Conclusion 204
    A Summary of Insights....................................205
    Strategies for Success....................................207
    Opportunities and a Roadmap for the Future .209
    Closing Thoughts 212
Author Bio...213
Acknowledgements 215
List of Books to Date 217
Social Profiles..220
Mentorship, Consulting and Public Speaking 221
I Value Your Feedback 223
  Updated Portfolio of Books...................................225

Introduction

Real estate and capital markets, two seemingly distinct worlds, yet intrinsically connected in ways that profoundly impact global economies, individual wealth, and investment strategies.

From towering skyscrapers financed by institutional investors to suburban homes influenced by mortgage-backed securities, the intersection of these domains is dynamic, evolving, and full of opportunities.

This book is an invitation to explore the bridge between capital markets and real estate, unraveling the complexities while empowering you with actionable insights.

In today's financial landscape, the integration of real estate and capital markets is undeniable. Real estate, long considered a stable asset class, has transformed from a primarily local business into a global investment opportunity driven by the sophisticated mechanisms of capital markets. On the flip side, capital markets leverage real estate's tangible and stable qualities to anchor portfolios, hedge risks, and diversify assets.

Understanding how these two forces interact is not just insightful, it's essential for anyone navigating investment strategies in a world where financial markets dictate so much of our economic reality.

The chapters ahead will guide you through this intricate relationship, starting with the fundamentals of capital markets and their role in the real estate ecosystem.

We'll examine financing methods, such as equity and debt, uncovering how instruments like Real Estate Investment Trusts (REITs) and mortgage-backed securities serve as crucial links between property and the financial world.

You'll gain insights into the role of institutional investors, the globalisation of real estate markets, and the economic indicators that shape these industries.

But this book is not merely an academic exploration, it is a practical roadmap. Whether you are an experienced investor, a real estate professional, or someone new to the field, the aim is to leave you equipped with strategies and a deeper understanding of how to integrate these markets into your financial decisions.

Each chapter builds upon the last, offering both theoretical knowledge and practical takeaways. For instance, you'll discover how to interpret market trends, mitigate risks, and leverage global opportunities, all while staying attuned to emerging technologies and sustainability efforts reshaping the industry.

Take a moment to reflect on your current understanding of real estate and capital markets. Perhaps you've wondered how institutional funds influence property values or how global economic shifts affect local real estate trends.

These questions are at the heart of this book. By exploring the interconnectedness of these markets, you'll uncover not just answers but actionable strategies tailored to today's fast-paced financial world.

The relationship between capital markets and real estate is a story of strategy. It is about positioning yourself where opportunity meets preparation. Imagine understanding the forces behind fluctuating property prices or grasping the dynamics of cross-border investments.

These insights are not just for academic circles, they are tools for building wealth, managing portfolios, and navigating risks with confidence.

In this chapter, we've introduced the core idea: bridging the gap between real estate and capital markets. This theme will flow through the book, providing context and clarity as we explore topics like equity financing, debt structures, and economic indicators.

The next chapter will delve deeper into the foundation of capital markets, where we'll break down the key components that drive their operation and set the stage for their role in real estate.

As you continue reading, I encourage you to approach the material with curiosity and reflection. Each chapter is a building block, offering insights that culminate in a comprehensive understanding of how capital markets and real estate are intricately woven together. By the end of this book, you'll have a clear vision of how to navigate these markets effectively, integrating strategy with opportunity.

Now, let's step forward into the world of capital markets and real estate, exploring the bridges that connect these vital forces in our economic landscape.

The journey begins here.

Chapter 1: Capital Market vs. Real Estate

Capital markets and real estate, two seemingly different worlds with their own languages, systems, and players.

Yet, at their core, these two industries share a relationship so intertwined that understanding one without the other can limit opportunities. Imagine a bridge where the flow of capital fuels the growth of cities, and the tangible security of real estate stabilises volatile financial markets.

This chapter introduces that bridge, shedding light on how these markets interact, thrive, and depend on each other. Whether you're a capital market specialist exploring new avenues or a real estate professional seeking to understand the forces shaping your industry, this chapter is your guide to uncovering these hidden connections.

The term "capital markets" might conjure images of stock tickers, trading floors, and financial reports. For the uninitiated, it can feel abstract and distant. In contrast, real estate, whether it's the house you live in or a towering office block, is tangible, rooted in the physical world. However, as we peel back the layers, the connection becomes clear: capital markets provide the financial lifeblood that real estate needs to grow, while real estate offers the stability and resilience that investors in capital markets crave.

Take, for example, a commercial development in a growing city. Before construction even begins, funding must be secured.

Equity financing might come from investors pooling money through Real Estate Investment Trusts (REITs), while debt financing might involve bonds issued in the capital markets. The completed property, once operational, might even be securitised, its future income sold to investors as mortgage-backed securities.

In this way, capital markets and real estate are part of a continuous cycle, one fueling the other.

Let's dive in.

The Tangible Meets the Financial

Real estate is often seen as a "safe haven" asset, prized for its stability during market fluctuations. In contrast, capital markets are known for their dynamism and liquidity.

The integration of these two worlds creates a synergy that benefits both industries. For investors in capital markets, real estate offers a way to diversify portfolios with tangible assets that can act as a hedge against inflation or economic downturns. For real estate professionals, capital markets unlock access to funding that can transform visions into reality.

The process is not without its complexities. A capital market specialist may need to understand the nuances of zoning laws, property valuations, and rental yields, while a real estate developer might need to grasp the fundamentals of interest rates, bond yields, and investor expectations. This integration requires a shared language, a strategic understanding of both realms.

This book serves to bridge that gap, providing insights and strategies for readers to navigate this intersection with confidence.

Investment as a Driving Force

At the heart of this relationship lies investment. Capital markets act as a global reservoir of funds, drawing from sources like institutional investors, mutual funds, and sovereign wealth funds.

These funds often flow into real estate, financing everything from residential developments to large-scale commercial projects. In return, real estate provides a steady stream of income through rents and leases, making it an attractive asset for investors seeking long-term returns.

But how does this work in practice? Imagine a pension fund looking for steady income to meet its obligations. Investing directly in property might be too hands-on, so the fund turns to REITs or bonds tied to real estate developments. These instruments offer exposure to real estate's benefits without the complexities of property management.

For the real estate industry, this creates a flow of capital that enables large-scale projects, driving growth and innovation.

Strategy at the Core

Both capital markets and real estate are built on strategy.

In real estate, this might involve choosing the right location, timing the market, or structuring deals to maximise returns. In capital markets, strategy revolves around analysing risk, balancing portfolios, and predicting market trends. When these strategies align, the results can be transformative.

Consider the globalisation of real estate markets. Capital from international investors flows across borders, funding developments in cities thousands of miles away. A capital market professional might assess opportunities in emerging markets, while a real estate developer considers how to attract foreign investment.

This dynamic interaction is both an opportunity and a challenge, requiring a deep understanding of market conditions, currency fluctuations, and regulatory environments.

Challenges and Opportunities

Of course, no relationship is without its challenges. The integration of real estate and capital markets introduces risks, from interest rate fluctuations to economic downturns.

Yet, these risks also create opportunities for those who can anticipate and navigate them. For example, during periods of economic uncertainty, capital might shift toward safer real estate investments, creating demand for high-quality assets. Conversely, in a booming economy, the availability of cheap debt can fuel rapid real estate expansion.

These dynamics are explored further in later chapters, where we'll delve into the intricacies of equity and debt financing, the role of institutional investors, and the impact of global trends on local markets.

Each chapter builds on the foundation laid here, providing practical takeaways and actionable insights tailored to both capital market specialists and real estate professionals.

A Partnership for the Future

The relationship between capital markets and real estate is not static, it evolves with technology, economic shifts, and changing investor preferences.

Emerging tools like blockchain and proptech are reshaping how properties are bought, sold, and financed. Sustainability is becoming a driving force, with investors prioritising green buildings and ESG (environmental, social, and governance) factors. These trends signal a future where the integration of capital markets and real estate will be more critical, and more innovative, than ever before.

As we move into the next chapter, we'll explore the foundation of capital markets, breaking down their structure and role in financing industries like real estate.

This deeper understanding will set the stage for navigating the complexities of these interconnected markets. For now, remember this: capital markets and real estate are two sides of the same coin, each amplifying the potential of the other.

Closing Thoughts

This chapter serves as your entry point into the dynamic world of capital markets and real estate.

By understanding their relationship, you unlock the potential to leverage one of the most powerful intersections in modern finance. As you continue reading, you'll gain the tools and strategies needed to navigate this space with confidence, whether your background is in financial markets or bricks and mortar.

The journey has just begun. Let's take the next step together and uncover how capital markets form the foundation of this extraordinary partnership.

Chapter 2: The Foundation of Capital Markets

Capital markets form the bedrock of modern global finance, acting as the vast and intricate network through which economies thrive and grow.

They serve as a meeting place for those who need money, governments, corporations, and real estate developers, and those who have money to invest. For centuries, capital markets have been the silent force behind innovation, infrastructure, and wealth creation.

Yet their significance is often overlooked, especially by those who are unfamiliar with their structure and role.

To fully grasp their importance, imagine a bustling marketplace, but instead of exchanging goods, participants trade financial instruments, bonds, equities, and derivatives.

These markets provide liquidity, enabling investors to buy and sell assets quickly without significantly affecting their price.

This liquidity is the lifeblood of capital markets, ensuring that money flows efficiently between participants.

In this chapter, we delve into the foundation of capital markets, unraveling their structure, their role in global finance, and their intrinsic connection to the real estate industry.

Let's continue.

Bonds and the Building Blocks of Capital

At the core of capital markets are bonds, often referred to as fixed-income securities.

Bonds represent debt; they are essentially loans that investors give to issuers like governments, municipalities, or corporations in exchange for regular interest payments and the return of the principal amount at maturity. Bonds are critical to capital markets because they provide a stable, predictable stream of income for investors and serve as a reliable source of funding for issuers.

For real estate, bonds play an indispensable role. Consider a city planning to expand its urban infrastructure with new residential developments, schools, and public transport systems.

Municipal bonds, often used to fund such projects, attract investors who are looking for low-risk, tax-efficient returns. Similarly, corporations involved in real estate development may issue corporate bonds to finance large-scale construction projects. This symbiotic relationship ensures that real estate development is fueled by the steady flow of capital from bond markets.

Equities: Ownership and Opportunity

Equities, or stocks, are another cornerstone of capital markets. Unlike bonds, which represent debt, equities signify ownership.

When you purchase shares in a company, you own a portion of that company and are entitled to a share of its profits through dividends, as well as potential capital gains if the company's value increases.

In the real estate context, equities play a transformative role, particularly through Real Estate Investment Trusts (REITs). REITs allow individuals to invest in real estate without directly owning property.

By buying shares in a REIT, investors gain access to a diversified portfolio of income-generating properties, ranging from office buildings and shopping centers to apartment complexes and industrial warehouses.

This equity-based approach democratizes real estate investment, opening doors for small investors while providing real estate developers with a steady influx of capital.

The trading of equities in capital markets is what drives liquidity, enabling investors to enter and exit positions with ease.

This liquidity is essential for REITs, as it provides investors with flexibility and confidence in their investments.

For the real estate industry, the equity market is not just a source of funding but also a gauge of market sentiment and economic health.

Trading and Market Dynamics

Trading is the lifeblood of capital markets. It is through trading that bonds, equities, and other financial instruments change hands, allowing markets to function efficiently.

Trading occurs in two primary forms: primary markets and secondary markets. In primary markets, new securities are issued and sold directly to investors, providing issuers with the capital they need. In secondary markets, previously issued securities are traded among investors, creating liquidity and price discovery.

Real estate developers often tap into primary markets to raise funds through initial public offerings (IPOs) of REITs or by issuing bonds. Meanwhile, secondary markets allow investors to trade these securities, ensuring that capital flows continuously.

The dynamic nature of trading also makes it possible to assess the health of the real estate market. For instance, rising REIT prices in secondary markets often indicate strong demand for real estate, while declining prices might signal investor caution.

Liquidity: The Engine of Efficiency

Liquidity is perhaps the most critical aspect of capital markets.

It is the measure of how easily an asset can be bought or sold without significantly affecting its price. Highly liquid markets, such as those for government bonds or large-cap equities, ensure that participants can trade efficiently, reducing transaction costs and risks.

For real estate, liquidity is both a challenge and an opportunity. Physical real estate assets are notoriously illiquid, they cannot be easily bought or sold, and transactions often involve high costs and lengthy processes. This is where capital markets bridge the gap. Instruments like REITs, mortgage-backed securities (MBS), and real estate mutual funds transform illiquid real estate into liquid assets that can be traded on public exchanges.

This liquidity attracts a broader pool of investors, ensuring that capital flows into real estate projects without the constraints of traditional property transactions.

Investors: The Lifeblood of Capital Markets

None of this would be possible without investors, the individuals, institutions, and entities that provide the capital fueling these markets.

Investors range from pension funds and insurance companies to retail investors and sovereign wealth funds.

Each group has unique objectives, risk tolerances, and investment horizons, shaping the dynamics of capital markets.

In the real estate sphere, institutional investors are particularly influential.

Their substantial capital resources enable them to invest in large-scale developments, purchase commercial properties, and support REITs.

For individual investors, capital markets offer indirect access to real estate through instruments like mutual funds and ETFs, which pool money from many investors to invest in diversified portfolios of real estate assets.

The role of investors in capital markets is not merely transactional, it is strategic.

By allocating capital to real estate projects, investors influence market trends, property values, and even urban development patterns.

For real estate professionals, understanding the motivations and strategies of these investors is essential for securing funding and aligning with market demands.

Interlinking with Real Estate

The connection between capital markets and real estate is more than financial, it is strategic.

Capital markets provide the mechanisms for raising funds, managing risks, and enabling liquidity, while real estate offers the tangible assets and income streams that attract capital.

This interdependence creates a feedback loop: strong real estate markets attract capital, and efficient capital markets fuel real estate growth.

For example, during periods of economic growth, low interest rates in bond markets often lead to increased real estate development, as developers can borrow at lower costs.

Conversely, during economic downturns, investors may flock to REITs and other real estate instruments as a safe haven, stabilizing property markets even in turbulent times.

Conclusion: The Foundation for Growth

Understanding the foundation of capital markets is essential for anyone navigating real estate investment. Bonds, equities, trading, liquidity, and investors are not just financial terms, they are the pillars supporting the real estate industry. By mastering these concepts, real estate professionals can access new funding sources, mitigate risks, and align their strategies with market dynamics.

As we move into the next chapter, we'll explore how these foundations translate into practical financing methods for real estate, from equity financing to the complexities of debt instruments. This knowledge will empower you to bridge the gap between the theoretical and the practical, unlocking the full potential of capital markets for real estate success.

The journey is just beginning. With a solid understanding of capital markets, you are now equipped to explore how these principles shape the world of real estate. Let's continue to build on this foundation and uncover the strategies that drive growth, innovation, and opportunity in both industries.

Chapter 3: Real Estate and Financial Ecosystems

Real estate is far more than physical structures or parcels of land; it is a cornerstone of the financial ecosystem.

From a capital market perspective, it serves as a robust and indispensable asset class.

For real estate professionals, understanding how their industry fits into the larger framework of global finance can unlock opportunities and broaden horizons.

Whether you're an investor diversifying a portfolio or a developer seeking funding, real estate's role in the financial ecosystem is one of stability, growth, and adaptability.

In this chapter, we explore how real estate functions as a critical part of investment portfolios and why its significance extends far beyond the physical realm.

We'll also examine the dynamics of diversification, portfolio allocation, and returns, while maintaining a balanced approach for readers who may come from one field but not the other.

For those steeped in real estate, this chapter will provide clarity on how your world connects with the financial ecosystem.

For capital markets specialists, it will demonstrate why real estate remains an essential piece of the investment puzzle.

Let's dive in.

Real Estate as an Asset Class

Real estate has long been recognised as one of the core asset classes in the financial ecosystem, alongside equities, bonds, and commodities.

Unlike other asset classes, however, real estate offers unique advantages that make it an enduring choice for investors. Its tangible nature provides a sense of security that stocks or bonds often cannot.

Furthermore, real estate's ability to generate consistent income through rents or leases adds an attractive layer of reliability to any portfolio.

For capital markets professionals, real estate offers a hedge against market volatility.

During economic downturns, when equities may falter, real estate often remains resilient. Conversely, for real estate professionals, the recognition of their industry as a bona fide asset class provides a direct link to the flow of global capital.

This dual perspective underscores why real estate is an indispensable component of the financial ecosystem.

One of real estate's most attractive features is its ability to deliver returns through two distinct channels: income and appreciation. Income is derived from rental yields or leases, providing steady cash flow for investors.

Appreciation, on the other hand, reflects the increase in property value over time.

Together, these two sources of returns make real estate a powerful contributor to portfolio performance.

Diversification: Spreading Risk

Diversification is one of the foundational principles of investing, and real estate plays a pivotal role in achieving it. In simple terms, diversification involves spreading investments across different asset classes to minimise risk. By including real estate in a portfolio, investors can reduce their exposure to the volatility of equities or the low yields of bonds.

Consider a pension fund managing billions in assets. While equities might offer growth potential and bonds provide stability, real estate acts as a stabiliser, offering a mix of income and long-term appreciation. Its relatively low correlation with other asset classes means that real estate often performs differently from stocks or bonds during market fluctuations, adding a layer of protection for investors.

For real estate professionals, understanding the concept of diversification is equally important. By positioning your projects or developments as low-risk, income-generating assets, you can attract institutional investors seeking to diversify their portfolios. This requires a strategic approach, including thorough market analysis, sustainable development practices, and a clear value proposition.

Portfolio Allocation: Striking the Right Balance

Portfolio allocation refers to the strategic distribution of investments across various asset classes to achieve specific financial goals. For many institutional investors, real estate represents a significant portion of their portfolio allocation. Studies have shown that including real estate can enhance returns while reducing overall portfolio risk, making it a crucial component of any well-balanced investment strategy.

Let's consider an example. A sovereign wealth fund managing a portfolio worth $500 billion might allocate 20% to equities, 30% to bonds, and 10% to real estate. This allocation reflects a calculated approach to balancing growth, stability, and income. The inclusion of real estate not only diversifies the portfolio but also ensures exposure to an asset class with unique characteristics, such as inflation protection and tangible value.

For capital markets specialists, understanding the nuances of portfolio allocation involving real estate can open doors to new investment opportunities. For real estate professionals, recognising how your projects fit into these broader strategies can help you tailor proposals to meet investor needs.

Returns: Measuring Success

At the heart of every investment decision lies the pursuit of returns.

For real estate, these returns come in two primary forms: income and capital appreciation. Income is generated through rental payments or leases, while capital appreciation reflects the increase in property value over time.

Together, these components make real estate an appealing choice for investors seeking steady, long-term gains.

In the context of the financial ecosystem, returns from real estate must be evaluated alongside those from other asset classes.

For instance, while equities might offer higher short-term gains, they come with increased volatility. Bonds, on the other hand, provide stability but often yield lower returns.

Real estate strikes a balance, offering a mix of stability and growth that appeals to a wide range of investors.

For capital markets professionals, analysing returns from real estate involves considering factors such as net operating income (NOI), cap rates, and cash-on-cash returns.

For real estate professionals, delivering these returns requires a focus on market trends, tenant retention, and efficient property management.

This interplay of financial and operational metrics underscores the importance of collaboration between these two worlds.

Real Estate's Role in the Financial Ecosystem

To understand real estate's place in the financial ecosystem, it's essential to view it as more than an isolated asset class.

Real estate connects with other parts of the financial system in numerous ways, from securitisation and mortgage markets to REITs and private equity funds. These connections create a dynamic feedback loop, where capital flows into real estate, generating returns that attract even more capital.

For instance, a commercial property in a major city might be financed through a mix of equity and debt, with shares traded on a public exchange. The income generated by that property could then be packaged into mortgage-backed securities, sold to investors seeking exposure to the real estate market. This cyclical process demonstrates how real estate functions not only as an investment opportunity but also as a vital component of the financial ecosystem.

Balancing Perspectives

At this stage in the book, readers may find themselves at different points of understanding.

For those with a real estate background, the financial terminology and concepts might feel unfamiliar or overwhelming. For capital markets professionals, the discussion of real estate may seem basic or overly simplified. Striking a balance between these perspectives is critical to bridging the gap between these two worlds.

For the real estate professional: Think of the financial ecosystem as the engine that powers your industry. Understanding its mechanisms can help you secure funding, attract investors, and position your projects for success.

For the capital markets specialist: Consider real estate not just as a physical asset but as a strategic tool within your portfolio. Its unique characteristics, stability, income generation, and low correlation with other assets, make it an invaluable addition to any investment strategy.

Conclusion: Real Estate as the Link

Real estate's role in the financial ecosystem is both profound and multifaceted.

It provides diversification, enhances portfolio performance, and offers unique returns that set it apart from other asset classes. At the same time, its integration with capital markets creates opportunities for innovation, collaboration, and growth.

As we move into the next chapter, we'll explore the methods of financing real estate through equity and debt. This will provide a deeper understanding of how real estate professionals and capital markets specialists can work together to create value and drive success. For now, remember that real estate is more than just an asset, it's a critical link in the financial ecosystem, connecting tangible properties with the flow of global capital.

The journey continues, and with each chapter, you'll gain a clearer picture of how these worlds interconnect. Let's move forward, building on this foundation to uncover the strategies that define success in real estate and capital markets alike.

Chapter 4: Equity Financing for Real Estate

Equity financing stands as one of the most dynamic and transformative forces in the real estate industry.

For centuries, individuals and institutions have pooled their resources to acquire and develop property, creating wealth and reshaping landscapes. In the financial ecosystem, equity financing represents the lifeblood of real estate, bridging investors with opportunities and unlocking the potential of tangible assets.

Whether you're a capital markets specialist exploring the intricacies of equity or a real estate professional seeking new avenues for funding, this chapter will provide a comprehensive understanding of how equity financing drives the real estate market forward.

Unlike debt financing, which relies on borrowing with the obligation to repay, equity financing involves raising capital through the sale of ownership stakes.

This means that equity investors share in both the risks and rewards of a project, making it a partnership rather than a liability.

The appeal of equity financing lies in its flexibility and potential for high returns, though it also comes with challenges and complexities that require careful navigation.

Let's continue.

What is Equity Financing?

Equity financing involves the exchange of capital for an ownership stake in a property or project. Investors provide funds without the expectation of immediate repayment, instead sharing in the profits, or losses, of the venture.

This form of financing is particularly attractive for large-scale developments, where traditional loans might fall short of covering the necessary capital.

For example, a real estate developer planning to build a luxury apartment complex might raise equity from a group of private investors. These investors, often referred to as equity partners, receive a proportional share of the project's profits in return for their capital contributions.

Unlike lenders, equity investors have no legal claim to the developer's personal assets, but they do take on a higher level of risk since their returns depend entirely on the project's success.

Real Estate Investment Trusts (REITs): Democratizing Equity Investment

One of the most significant advancements in equity financing is the rise of Real Estate Investment Trusts (REITs).

REITs allow individuals to invest in real estate without directly owning property, providing exposure to a diversified portfolio of income-generating assets.

These publicly traded entities have transformed the real estate industry by making it accessible to retail investors while offering developers a steady flow of capital.

For the real estate professional, REITs represent an opportunity to scale projects and attract institutional investors. For the capital markets specialist, they serve as a vehicle for integrating real estate into broader investment portfolios.

The liquidity of REIT shares, combined with their regular dividend payouts, makes them an attractive option for both parties.

Consider the example of a REIT focused on commercial office spaces.

By pooling funds from thousands of investors, the REIT can acquire, develop, and manage properties that would be out of reach for individual investors.

The income generated from tenant leases is distributed as dividends, creating a steady stream of returns.

For developers, this arrangement eliminates the need to manage individual investors while ensuring a consistent capital flow.

Private Equity in Real Estate

While REITs dominate the public equity space, private equity plays an equally important role in real estate financing. Private equity funds are pools of capital collected from high-net-worth individuals, institutional investors, and even family offices. These funds target specific types of real estate investments, ranging from distressed properties to luxury developments.

Private equity offers a more hands-on approach than REITs, often involving direct participation in the management and development of properties. For real estate professionals, partnering with private equity funds can provide access to significant capital resources, along with the expertise and networks of seasoned investors. However, this type of financing comes with high expectations, as private equity investors typically demand strong returns within a defined timeframe.

For capital markets specialists, private equity funds in real estate present an opportunity to invest in niche markets or underutilised properties. The ability to identify undervalued assets and transform them into profitable ventures underscores the strategic potential of private equity in the real estate ecosystem.

Crowdfunding and Syndication: The New Frontier

In recent years, technology has disrupted traditional equity financing methods, giving rise to crowdfunding platforms and syndication models.

These innovative approaches democratise real estate investment, allowing individuals to participate in projects with relatively small capital contributions.

Crowdfunding platforms connect developers with a broad audience of potential investors, often through online portals.

For example, a developer planning a boutique hotel might use a crowdfunding platform to raise equity from hundreds of small investors, each contributing as little as $1,000.

This model not only expands the pool of potential investors but also allows developers to maintain greater control over their projects.

Syndication, on the other hand, involves pooling resources from a smaller group of investors, often facilitated by a syndicator or sponsor.

This model is particularly popular for commercial real estate projects, where the capital requirements are significant.

For investors, syndication offers an opportunity to participate in large-scale developments without the complexities of direct ownership.

For both real estate professionals and capital markets specialists, these new models of equity financing represent a paradigm shift, making real estate investment more inclusive and accessible.

The Role of Equity in Portfolio Diversification

From the perspective of capital markets, equity financing in real estate is a powerful tool for diversification. By including real estate equity in their portfolios, investors can achieve a balance between risk and reward, benefiting from the stability of physical assets and the growth potential of the real estate market.

For example, a pension fund might allocate a portion of its portfolio to REITs or private equity real estate funds. These investments provide exposure to income-generating properties while hedging against inflation and market volatility. The low correlation between real estate and other asset classes, such as equities and bonds, enhances overall portfolio performance, making real estate equity a cornerstone of diversification strategies.

For real estate professionals, understanding the importance of diversification is crucial when pitching projects to investors. By positioning your development as a strategic addition to an investment portfolio, you can attract equity partners who value the stability and returns offered by real estate.

Challenges and Risks in Equity Financing

Despite its many advantages, equity financing comes with its own set of challenges and risks. For developers, the dilution of ownership is a significant consideration. By raising capital through equity, you are effectively sharing control of your project with investors, which can lead to conflicts over decision-making and strategy.

For investors, the primary risk lies in the performance of the underlying property or project. Unlike debt financing, where returns are fixed, equity returns depend entirely on the success of the investment. This makes due diligence and market analysis critical for both parties.

Economic conditions also play a significant role in the viability of equity financing. During periods of economic uncertainty, raising equity can become more challenging as investors seek safer, more liquid options. Conversely, in a booming market, the availability of equity can drive rapid real estate expansion, creating opportunities for those prepared to capitalise on them.

Conclusion: The Power of Equity

Equity financing is more than just a means of raising capital, it is a strategic partnership that aligns the interests of developers and investors. From REITs and private equity funds to crowdfunding platforms and syndication models, equity financing offers a range of options to suit different types of real estate projects and investors.

For capital markets specialists, real estate equity provides an avenue for diversification, stability, and long-term returns. For real estate professionals, it is a tool for turning ambitious visions into reality. By understanding the nuances of equity financing, both groups can unlock new opportunities and navigate the complexities of the real estate financial ecosystem.

As we move into the next chapter, we'll explore the other side of the coin: debt financing. Together, equity and debt form the foundation of real estate finance, providing the resources and strategies needed to build and grow. Let's continue this journey, uncovering the tools and insights that drive success in real estate and capital markets.

Chapter 5: Debt Financing in Real Estate

Debt financing serves as the backbone of real estate funding, enabling projects of all sizes to come to life, from the construction of towering skyscrapers to the purchase of a family home.

While equity financing, as discussed in the previous chapter, is about ownership and shared risk, debt financing is fundamentally about borrowing.

It allows individuals and entities to leverage their resources, using borrowed capital to achieve goals that might otherwise be unattainable.

Mortgages, bonds, and other debt instruments form the core of this system, creating opportunities for growth while also introducing layers of complexity and risk.

In this chapter, we will explore how debt financing operates within real estate markets, the critical role it plays in connecting capital markets to real estate, and how instruments like mortgages and bonds serve as vital links.

As we build on the foundational concepts from Chapters 1 through 4, we'll see how debt financing complements equity, contributing to the financial ecosystem that fuels real estate development and investment.

We'll also hint at future discussions on risk management and innovative financing solutions to ensure a comprehensive understanding of this crucial topic.

Let's begin.

The Role of Mortgages in Real Estate

Mortgages are perhaps the most familiar form of debt financing in real estate.

For individuals, a mortgage is the key to homeownership, providing the capital needed to purchase property while spreading the cost over time.

For real estate developers, commercial mortgages offer a similar function, enabling the acquisition and development of land and buildings.

Mortgages are not just loans, they are strategic tools that allow real estate transactions to flourish while maintaining liquidity for both buyers and lenders.

A mortgage, in its simplest form, is a secured loan where the property itself serves as collateral. This structure creates a symbiotic relationship: the borrower gains access to capital, while the lender secures their investment against the property's value.

The importance of mortgages to the real estate market cannot be overstated; they make real estate accessible to a broader audience, driving demand and fueling growth.

From a capital markets perspective, mortgages play a pivotal role as well. Mortgage-backed securities

(MBS), which bundle individual loans into tradable financial instruments, are a prime example of how debt financing links real estate to global finance.

By converting illiquid mortgages into liquid securities, capital markets provide lenders with the ability to recycle funds, extending new loans and keeping the market active.

Bonds: Bridging Real Estate and Capital Markets

While mortgages dominate individual real estate transactions, bonds are the lifeblood of large-scale real estate financing.

Bonds are essentially loans issued by governments, municipalities, or corporations, where investors provide capital in exchange for periodic interest payments and the return of the principal upon maturity. In real estate, bonds can take many forms, each tailored to specific needs.

Municipal bonds, for example, are often used to fund infrastructure projects that support real estate development, such as roads, schools, and utilities.

Corporate bonds, issued by real estate companies or developers, provide the capital needed for large-scale construction or acquisitions.

These bonds are then traded on capital markets, linking real estate funding directly to global investors.

One of the key benefits of bonds in real estate financing is their scalability.

Unlike mortgages, which are typically tied to individual properties, bonds can finance multi-billion-dollar projects, making them indispensable for large-scale urban development.

For capital markets specialists, bonds represent a relatively stable investment, often secured by the income generated from the underlying real estate assets.

Debt Instruments: Beyond Mortgages and Bonds

While mortgages and bonds are the most prominent forms of debt financing, other instruments play critical roles in the real estate ecosystem. Mezzanine financing, for example, sits between equity and traditional debt, offering higher returns to lenders in exchange for increased risk. In real estate, mezzanine loans are often used to fill funding gaps, providing developers with the additional capital needed to complete projects.

Another key instrument is construction loans, short-term debt used to fund the construction phase of a project. Unlike traditional mortgages, construction loans are disbursed in stages, aligned with the project's progress. These loans are typically replaced with long-term financing upon project completion, creating a seamless transition from development to operation.

Real estate professionals and capital markets specialists alike must understand the interplay between these instruments. Each serves a specific purpose, and together, they create a financing ecosystem that supports real estate at every stage, from acquisition and development to long-term management.

The Cost of Borrowing: Interest Rates and Debt Sustainability

At the heart of debt financing lies the concept of interest, the cost of borrowing capital.

Interest rates, influenced by central banks, inflation, and market dynamics, are a critical factor in determining the viability of real estate projects.

Low interest rates, for example, make borrowing more affordable, driving demand for real estate and spurring development.

Conversely, high interest rates can dampen activity, as the cost of servicing debt becomes prohibitive.

For real estate professionals, managing the cost of borrowing is an essential skill. Fixed-rate and variable-rate loans offer different advantages and risks, and selecting the right option requires careful analysis.

For capital markets specialists, interest rates provide a barometer of economic health, influencing investment decisions and portfolio strategies.

Debt sustainability is another crucial consideration. While leveraging debt can amplify returns, excessive borrowing introduces significant risks.

A project with unsustainable debt levels may struggle to generate sufficient income to cover interest payments, leading to financial distress or even default.

For both borrowers and lenders, maintaining a balance between ambition and prudence is key to long-term success.

Debt Financing's Link to Capital Markets

As discussed in Chapter 2, capital markets provide the platform through which debt instruments are traded, creating liquidity and connecting real estate to global investors.

Mortgage-backed securities, corporate bonds, and even mezzanine loans are all examples of how debt financing ties real estate to the broader financial ecosystem.

For real estate professionals, this connection offers access to a vast pool of capital, enabling projects that might otherwise be out of reach. For capital markets specialists, real estate debt instruments provide opportunities for diversification, stability, and income generation.

This interplay underscores the importance of understanding both sides of the equation, as success often depends on the ability to navigate these interconnected markets.

Balancing Perspectives

At this stage, readers may find themselves grappling with different challenges.

For those from a real estate background, the complexities of debt instruments and their links to capital markets might seem overwhelming. For capital markets specialists, the nuances of real estate financing may feel overly detailed or even unnecessary.

For the real estate professional: Think of debt financing as the engine that powers your projects. Understanding the tools and strategies available can help you secure funding, manage costs, and position your developments for success.

For the capital markets specialist: Consider real estate debt instruments not just as assets, but as opportunities to connect with tangible, income-generating projects. By exploring these instruments, you can align your strategies with the stability and growth potential of the real estate market.

Conclusion: Building on Debt

Debt financing is a cornerstone of real estate markets, providing the capital needed to fuel growth and innovation.

From mortgages and bonds to mezzanine loans and construction financing, debt instruments create opportunities for both developers and investors.

By linking real estate to capital markets, these tools ensure that the flow of capital continues, enabling projects that shape our cities and communities.

As we move into the next chapter, we'll explore the role of institutional investors in real estate, examining how their capital and strategies influence markets on a global scale. Together, equity and debt form the foundation of real estate finance, but it is the participation of institutional players that truly transforms the industry.

Let's continue to uncover the connections and strategies that drive success in real estate and capital markets.

Chapter 6: The Role of Institutional Capital

Institutional investors, such as pension funds, insurance companies, and sovereign wealth funds, play an essential role in shaping the real estate market.

These large-scale players manage vast pools of capital, directing their investments toward opportunities that promise stability, long-term returns, and portfolio diversification.

For real estate professionals, institutional capital represents a lifeline for funding large-scale developments.

For capital markets specialists, it provides a connection to the tangible, income-generating assets that define real estate's role in the global financial ecosystem.

This chapter delves into the impact of institutional capital on real estate, connecting the dots between previous discussions on the foundations of capital markets (Chapter 2), equity and debt financing (Chapters 4 and 5), and the financial ecosystem of real estate (Chapter 3).

By exploring how institutional investors operate, their strategic motivations, and their influence on global markets, we aim to bridge the knowledge gap for both real estate and capital markets audiences.

Let's dive in.

What is Institutional Capital?

Institutional capital refers to the substantial financial resources managed by organisations like pension funds, insurance companies, and sovereign wealth funds.

These entities act on behalf of their beneficiaries, deploying funds in a way that balances risk with reward while maintaining a focus on long-term growth.

For example, a pension fund might allocate a portion of its portfolio to real estate investments to generate steady income through rents and leases. Sovereign wealth funds, often managing the financial assets of entire nations, frequently invest in large-scale real estate projects as a means of stabilising and diversifying their portfolios.

These investments can take many forms, from direct property acquisitions to participation in private equity real estate funds or publicly traded Real Estate Investment Trusts (REITs).

Pension Funds: Long-Term Stability

Pension funds are among the most influential institutional investors in real estate.

Their investment strategies are driven by the need to meet the long-term obligations of providing retirement income to their members. Real estate aligns perfectly with these goals, offering consistent rental yields and the potential for capital appreciation over extended periods.

Consider the role of pension funds in financing commercial properties, such as office buildings or multifamily housing developments. These assets are carefully selected for their ability to generate reliable income streams over decades. For real estate developers, attracting pension fund investment often requires demonstrating not only financial viability but also a commitment to sustainable, future-proofed projects that align with long-term market trends.

Insurance Companies: Balancing Risk and Returns

Insurance companies, another major player in the institutional capital space, manage significant reserves that must remain accessible to cover potential claims.

This need for liquidity and stability makes real estate an attractive investment option. Income-producing properties, such as retail centres, industrial warehouses, or healthcare facilities, often fit neatly into an insurance company's portfolio strategy.

Beyond direct property ownership, insurance companies also participate in real estate-backed financial instruments, such as mortgage-backed securities (MBS). These securities, discussed in Chapter 5, offer a way for insurers to diversify their exposure while benefiting from the stability of real estate cash flows. For developers and real estate professionals, understanding the preferences of insurance companies can open doors to funding opportunities, especially for projects that align with risk-averse investment profiles.

Sovereign Wealth Funds: Global Reach

Sovereign wealth funds (SWFs) manage the financial assets of nations, often derived from surplus revenues like oil exports or trade surpluses.

With their long-term investment horizons, SWFs are well-suited to real estate, which offers the combination of income, capital growth, and stability they require.

These funds frequently target high-profile, income-generating properties in major global cities or invest in large-scale urban developments that align with their strategic goals. For example, SWFs often prioritise properties with green building certifications or developments in emerging markets, reflecting their commitment to sustainable growth and diversification.

For real estate professionals, collaborating with SWFs demands a deep understanding of market trends, governance standards, and global investment strategies.

Private Equity Funds: Strategic Partners

Private equity real estate funds, as discussed in Chapter 4, are another critical vehicle for institutional capital.

These funds pool resources from multiple institutional investors to target real estate opportunities with high growth potential. Unlike more passive investments, private equity funds typically take a hands-on approach, focusing on value-add or opportunistic strategies that aim to transform underperforming assets into high-yield properties.

For real estate developers, partnering with private equity funds offers access to substantial financial resources and strategic guidance. However, these partnerships often come with stringent performance expectations and tight timelines for delivering returns.

For capital markets specialists, private equity funds represent an opportunity to invest in innovative projects that may fall outside the scope of traditional investments.

Practical Examples: Institutional Capital in Action

Institutional capital's influence on real estate markets can be seen in a variety of contexts, from stabilising urban housing markets to funding large-scale infrastructure developments.

For example, pension funds frequently invest in mixed-use developments that integrate residential, commercial, and retail spaces, creating vibrant, self-sustaining communities.

These projects are carefully designed to generate consistent income while supporting local economic growth.

Similarly, insurance companies often target niche markets, such as senior living facilities or student housing, which offer stable demand and predictable cash flows.

By aligning their investments with demographic trends, these institutions ensure a steady return on investment while addressing critical societal needs.

Sovereign wealth funds, meanwhile, play a pivotal role in emerging markets.

By investing in rapidly growing cities, these funds drive urbanisation, create jobs, and establish critical infrastructure.

For real estate professionals in these regions, attracting SWF investment requires a clear understanding of local market dynamics and the ability to present projects that align with the fund's strategic objectives.

.

Balancing Perspectives

As we continue to explore the interplay between capital markets and real estate, it's important to address the differing perspectives of our readers. For those with a real estate background, the scale and complexity of institutional investments might seem overwhelming. For capital markets specialists, the operational nuances of real estate may feel secondary to financial metrics.

For real estate professionals: View institutional investors not just as sources of capital, but as strategic partners who can provide stability, guidance, and market insights. Aligning your projects with their long-term goals is key to building successful relationships.

For capital markets specialists: Recognise real estate as more than an asset class, it is a platform for achieving portfolio diversification, stabilising returns, and driving impact.

Understanding the intricacies of real estate markets enhances your ability to identify and capitalise on opportunities.

Conclusion: A Foundation for Growth

Institutional capital is a cornerstone of the real estate market, driving growth, innovation, and stability. Whether through direct property ownership, participation in REITs, or investments in private equity funds, institutional investors shape the built environment and influence market trends on a global scale.

As we move into the next chapter, we'll examine the role of global trends and cross-border investments in real estate, exploring how international capital flows are reshaping the industry. By understanding the strategies and motivations of institutional investors, you are better equipped to navigate the dynamic relationship between real estate and capital markets.

The journey continues, uncovering the connections and strategies that define success in this evolving ecosystem.

Let's move forward, building on the foundation of institutional capital to explore the global opportunities ahead.

Chapter 7: Securitization and Real Estate

Imagine a world where loans tied to properties, be they residential mortgages or commercial real estate loans, are not merely contracts between lenders and borrowers but instead transformed into financial products traded on global markets.

This is the world of securitization, a revolutionary financial mechanism that bridges real estate and capital markets, providing liquidity, diversification, and opportunities for both industries.

Securitization has reshaped the real estate landscape, turning once-illiquid assets into tradable securities, driving funding efficiencies, and enabling vast capital flows into real estate projects.

For real estate professionals, it offers a powerful tool for accessing funding, while for capital markets specialists, it opens up an array of investment opportunities tied to tangible, income-generating assets.

However, securitization is not without its complexities or risks, and understanding its mechanics is essential for leveraging its benefits effectively.

In this chapter, we break down the process of securitizing mortgages, its impact on both real estate and financial markets, and its role in the broader economic ecosystem.

Building on foundational concepts from Chapters 1 through 6, we will explore the intricate connections between securitization, debt financing, institutional capital, and the financial ecosystem, while also setting the stage for future discussions on market trends and risk management.

Let's begin.

What is Securitization?

At its core, securitization is the process of pooling together loans or other income-generating assets and transforming them into tradable securities. These securities, often referred to as mortgage-backed securities (MBS) in the context of real estate, are then sold to investors in the capital markets.

For example, a bank that originates mortgages might bundle hundreds or thousands of these loans into a single pool. This pool is then structured into securities that represent claims on the cash flows generated by the underlying mortgages, namely, the monthly payments made by borrowers. These securities are sold to investors, providing the bank with immediate capital to issue more loans.

The beauty of securitization lies in its ability to create liquidity. Mortgages, which are typically long-term, illiquid assets, are transformed into securities that can be bought and sold on secondary markets. This process connects the real estate industry to global capital markets, ensuring a steady flow of funding for both residential and commercial properties.

How Securitization Works

The securitization process is a complex system involving multiple players and steps, each contributing to the transformation of loans into marketable securities.

It begins with originators, typically banks or financial institutions, that create the loans, such as mortgages, that serve as the foundation for securitization.

These loans are then bundled into a pool, forming a large, diversified portfolio of assets. To facilitate the securitization, the pooled loans are transferred to a Special Purpose Vehicle (SPV), a legally distinct entity designed to hold the assets and issue securities.

This transfer ensures the loans are isolated from the originator's balance sheet, reducing financial risk.

The process continues with tranching, where the pool is divided into layers based on risk and return. Senior tranches carry lower risk and offer lower returns, while junior tranches involve higher risk but promise greater yields.

The SPV then issues securities backed by the cash flows generated by the pooled loans, selling them to investors in capital markets.

Finally, loan servicers play a critical role by collecting payments from borrowers and distributing these funds to investors in accordance with the terms of the securities.

This systematic approach transforms traditional loans into investment opportunities, bridging borrowers and investors through the capital markets.

This structure, while complex, enables the seamless flow of capital between real estate and financial markets, aligning the interests of borrowers, lenders, and investors.

The Role of Mortgage-Backed Securities (MBS)

Mortgage-backed securities are the most common product of securitization in the real estate market.

These instruments allow investors to gain exposure to real estate without directly owning properties. For example, an investor who purchases an MBS is essentially buying a share of the cash flows generated by a pool of mortgages.

Mortgage-Backed Securities (MBS) are broadly categorised into two primary forms, each serving distinct investment needs and risk profiles.

Residential Mortgage-Backed Securities (RMBS) are backed by residential mortgages and are generally considered lower-risk investments. They offer steady and predictable returns, making them appealing to conservative investors.

On the other hand, Commercial Mortgage-Backed Securities (CMBS) are backed by loans on commercial properties. These securities often carry higher risk due to the complexities and market volatility associated with commercial real estate. However, they can also provide investors with the potential for higher returns, particularly in robust or growing markets.

Together, RMBS and CMBS offer a spectrum of opportunities for investors to diversify their portfolios within the realm of real estate finance.

For real estate professionals, MBS provide a pathway to increased funding for projects.

By securitizing loans, banks and lenders can free up capital to issue more loans, driving growth in the real estate market.

For capital markets specialists, MBS offer a diversified investment opportunity with predictable cash flows.

Benefits of Securitization

Securitization provides significant benefits that impact both real estate and financial markets, creating value for various stakeholders. One key advantage is liquidity; by transforming traditionally illiquid assets like mortgages into tradable securities, securitization ensures a continuous flow of capital. This enhanced liquidity is particularly valuable during times of economic uncertainty, as explored in Chapters 2 and 5. Additionally, securitization facilitates risk diversification by distributing risks among a wide range of investors, thereby reducing the concentration of risk for any single entity.

For lenders, securitization improves funding efficiency by recycling capital, allowing them to issue more loans and fuel increased real estate activity. Meanwhile, for investors, securitized products open the door to real estate markets without the complexities and challenges associated with direct ownership. These structured investment opportunities enable participation in a traditionally asset-intensive market, offering both accessibility and flexibility. Collectively, these benefits underline the importance of securitization as a transformative mechanism in the intersection of real estate and finance.

Challenges and Risks

While securitization offers significant advantages, it also introduces a range of risks and challenges that must be carefully managed.

One major concern is the complexity of securitized products, which can be difficult for some investors to fully comprehend. This complexity may act as a barrier, limiting accessibility to only those with advanced financial knowledge.

Furthermore, the value of securitized products is highly sensitive to broader market conditions, such as fluctuations in interest rates and economic trends, as discussed in Chapter 3.

This market volatility can lead to unpredictable performance and heightened investment risk.

Another critical issue is moral hazard, which arises from the separation of loan origination and risk retention. This disconnect can incentivise irresponsible lending practices, as was evident during the 2008 financial crisis.

Originators, lacking direct exposure to the risks of default, may prioritise volume over quality, ultimately destabilising the financial system.

These risks highlight the need for robust regulatory oversight and informed decision-making to ensure securitization remains a beneficial tool in both the real estate and financial markets.

For both real estate professionals and capital markets specialists, navigating these risks requires a deep understanding of market dynamics, regulatory frameworks, and the underlying assets.

Practical Examples of Securitization

To illustrate the impact of securitization, consider the case of a residential housing boom in a growing city.

Banks originating home loans can bundle these mortgages into RMBS, selling them to investors worldwide. This process not only provides funding for more homebuyers but also connects local real estate markets to global capital flows.

On the commercial side, a large-scale retail development might be funded through loans that are later securitized into CMBS.

These securities attract institutional investors seeking exposure to commercial real estate, creating a win-win scenario for developers and investors alike.

Building on Earlier Chapters

Securitization ties together many of the themes explored in earlier chapters.

From the foundational role of capital markets (Chapter 2) to the mechanisms of debt financing (Chapter 5), securitization serves as a bridge that connects these concepts. By understanding how loans are transformed into marketable securities, both real estate professionals and capital markets specialists can appreciate the interconnectedness of these industries.

Looking Ahead

As we move forward, the focus will shift to global trends in real estate capital markets, exploring how cross-border investments and emerging markets are reshaping the industry. Securitization, as a tool for connecting real estate to global capital, will remain a central theme, influencing everything from market dynamics to risk management strategies.

Conclusion: Unlocking Potential

Securitization is a cornerstone of modern real estate finance, providing the liquidity, diversification, and efficiency needed to drive growth and innovation. By transforming loans into tradable securities, it bridges the gap between real estate and capital markets, creating opportunities for all participants.

For real estate professionals, understanding securitization is key to accessing funding and navigating market trends. For capital markets specialists, it offers a pathway to diversified, income-generating investments tied to tangible assets.

The journey continues, uncovering the strategies and tools that define success in real estate and capital markets. Let's move forward, building on the insights gained here to explore the global opportunities that lie ahead.

Chapter 8: Private vs. Public Real Estate Market

The real estate market operates on two distinct fronts: the private market, where individual deals and niche investments dominate, and the public market, where broad access and liquidity prevail.

Each of these markets offers unique opportunities and challenges, catering to different investor profiles and strategic goals.

For real estate professionals, understanding the nuances of private and public markets can unlock funding sources and guide decision-making.

For those employed in capital markets or working within the real estate divisions of financial institutions, appreciating the interplay between these markets is essential for crafting informed investment strategies.

This chapter compares private equity real estate and public real estate markets, exploring their structures, investment approaches, and impacts on the broader financial ecosystem.

Building on previous discussions about equity financing (Chapter 4), institutional capital (Chapter 6), and securitization (Chapter 7), we'll delve into how private and public markets intersect, complement, and compete.

The aim is to provide a comprehensive understanding for all readers, whether they are seasoned professionals or newcomers seeking insights into how these two worlds operate and converge.

Let's continue.

Understanding Private Real Estate Markets

The private real estate market is characterised by its exclusivity, flexibility, and tailored investment strategies.

Transactions occur directly between buyers and sellers, often facilitated by private equity funds, family offices, or individual investors. Unlike public markets, where assets are traded on exchanges, private market investments are negotiated deals involving tangible properties or limited ownership stakes.

Private markets offer a high degree of customisation. Investors can target specific asset types, locations, or development stages, allowing them to align investments with their unique goals.

For example, a private equity real estate fund might focus on value-add projects, acquiring underperforming properties with the intent to enhance their value through renovations or operational improvements.

These funds often have more control over the assets they manage, enabling active involvement in property management and strategic decision-making.

One of the defining features of private real estate markets is their illiquidity.

Unlike public markets, where securities can be bought and sold with ease, private real estate investments typically require long holding periods.

This illiquidity, however, comes with potential rewards, as private market investments often yield higher returns due to the risks and complexities involved.

Public Real Estate Markets: Accessibility and Liquidity

In contrast, the public real estate market offers broad access and liquidity, making it an attractive option for institutional and retail investors alike.

Publicly traded Real Estate Investment Trusts (REITs) are the cornerstone of this market, providing investors with exposure to real estate assets without the challenges of direct ownership. REITs pool capital from numerous investors to acquire and manage income-generating properties, distributing profits as dividends.

Public markets are defined by transparency. Securities are traded on exchanges, providing real-time pricing and detailed disclosures about the underlying assets.

This transparency attracts a diverse range of investors, from individuals seeking passive income to large institutions looking to diversify portfolios.

The liquidity of public markets is another significant advantage. Investors can buy or sell shares in REITs or real estate-related stocks with minimal transaction costs, allowing them to adjust their exposure to real estate quickly. This flexibility makes public markets particularly appealing during periods of economic uncertainty or market volatility, as discussed in Chapter 2.

While public markets offer convenience and accessibility, they also come with certain limitations. Returns are often influenced by market sentiment and macroeconomic factors, making them more volatile than private market investments.

Additionally, public market investors have less control over the management and operations of the underlying assets, relying instead on the expertise of REIT managers or corporate executives.

Comparing Investment Strategies

The investment strategies employed in private and public real estate markets differ significantly, reflecting the unique characteristics of each.

In private markets, the focus is often on active value creation. Investors engage directly with properties, identifying opportunities to enhance value through renovations, operational efficiencies, or strategic repositioning.

This hands-on approach requires a deep understanding of local markets, regulatory environments, and tenant needs. For capital markets professionals working within real estate divisions, private market investments offer opportunities to structure complex deals and leverage expertise to generate alpha.

Public markets, by contrast, emphasise passive income and portfolio diversification.

REITs, for example, provide exposure to a diversified portfolio of properties, reducing risk while generating steady cash flows through dividend distributions. For real estate professionals, public markets offer a way to scale projects and access capital from a broad investor base.

For capital markets specialists, they provide a transparent and liquid means of integrating real estate into multi-asset portfolios.

Both markets play a critical role in the broader financial ecosystem.

Private markets drive innovation and development, creating opportunities for value creation and strategic growth.

Public markets, on the other hand, provide stability and liquidity, enabling investors to participate in real estate with lower barriers to entry.

Practical Examples

To illustrate the differences between private and public real estate markets, consider the example of a luxury hotel development.

In the private market, a real estate developer might partner with a private equity fund to finance the project.

This partnership allows for a tailored approach, with the fund providing not only capital but also strategic guidance on design, operations, and marketing.

The project is managed with a focus on maximising its unique value proposition, often involving direct negotiations with contractors, local authorities, and tenants.

In the public market, a REIT specialising in hospitality properties might acquire the completed hotel, integrating it into its portfolio of income-generating assets. Investors in the REIT benefit from the property's cash flows without the complexities of direct ownership. This transition from private development to public ownership highlights how these markets complement each other, each serving distinct investor needs.

Another example is the redevelopment of urban office spaces into mixed-use developments.

In the private market, this process might involve securing capital from multiple private investors, each with a stake in the project's success.

In the public market, a REIT or real estate-focused exchange-traded fund (ETF) could provide exposure to the finished development, offering investors access to its long-term income potential.

These examples underscore the interconnectedness of private and public markets, illustrating how capital flows between the two to support real estate's growth and evolution.

Balancing Perspectives

At this stage in the book, it's essential to address the perspectives of readers from different backgrounds. For those employed in the real estate sector, understanding the nuances of public markets can open new avenues for funding and collaboration. For capital markets professionals, gaining insights into private real estate investments can enhance portfolio strategies and decision-making.

For real estate professionals: Think of public markets as a gateway to scalability. By positioning your projects to attract REITs or other publicly traded entities, you can tap into a global investor base while maintaining focus on your core expertise.

For capital markets specialists: Recognise the potential of private markets to generate alpha through active value creation. By exploring opportunities in private equity real estate, you can uncover unique investments that complement broader portfolio objectives.

Looking Ahead

As we transition into the next chapter, the focus will shift to the globalisation of real estate markets, examining how cross-border investments and international capital flows are reshaping the industry. The interplay between private and public markets will remain a central theme, influencing how real estate adapts to global trends and challenges.

Conclusion: Two Markets, One Ecosystem

Private and public real estate markets operate on different principles, yet they are deeply interconnected, forming a cohesive ecosystem that drives growth, innovation, and investment. For real estate professionals, understanding these markets offers a pathway to accessing diverse funding sources and scaling projects effectively. For those in capital markets, they provide complementary opportunities to balance risk and reward.

As we move forward, the dynamic interplay between private and public markets will continue to shape the future of real estate finance. By leveraging the insights gained in this chapter, you are better equipped to navigate these two worlds, unlocking opportunities that align with your strategic goals.

The journey continues, exploring the global forces that define success in real estate and capital markets. Let's move forward, building on this foundation to uncover the trends and strategies that will shape the industry's future.

Chapter 9: Economic Indicators

Economic indicators are the compass by which investors, developers, and policymakers navigate the complexities of capital markets and real estate. Gross Domestic Product (GDP), inflation, and interest rates are among the most influential metrics, shaping decisions that impact portfolios, projects, and entire economies.

Understanding these indicators is not just an academic exercise, it's a strategic necessity for anyone involved in real estate or capital markets.

This chapter explores how these key economic indicators influence both markets, highlighting the intricate connections between GDP growth, inflationary pressures, and interest rate movements. For readers who wish to delve deeper into the foundational principles of real estate economics, I encourage you to refer to my previous book, *Real Estate Economics: Property, Markets, Principles, and Practices*. That book provides a detailed framework for understanding how economic theories apply to real estate, offering a valuable complement to the practical insights provided here.

Our goal in this chapter is twofold: to make economic terminology accessible to real estate professionals and to bridge the gap for capital markets specialists by demonstrating how these indicators influence real estate markets.

By the end, you'll have a clearer understanding of the forces at play and their implications for both industries.

Let's dive in.

GDP: The Pulse of Economic Health

Gross Domestic Product (GDP) measures the total value of goods and services produced within a country over a specific period.

As a broad indicator of economic health, GDP growth signals expanding markets and rising demand, while GDP contraction often points to economic slowdowns or recessions.

For real estate, GDP is a key driver of market dynamics. When GDP grows, businesses expand, employment rises, and consumer spending increases, all of which create demand for commercial and residential properties.

Office spaces fill as companies hire more workers, retail properties thrive as consumer confidence boosts spending, and residential markets flourish as incomes rise.

Conversely, when GDP contracts, the ripple effects can be felt across the real estate sector.

Companies may downsize, leading to increased office vacancies. Consumer spending may decline, affecting retail spaces. Homebuyers may hesitate, impacting residential sales.

For developers, GDP trends serve as a vital indicator for planning new projects and assessing market risk.

From a capital markets perspective, GDP growth is closely tied to the performance of equities, bonds, and other financial instruments. Rising GDP often correlates with higher corporate profits, buoying stock markets.

However, it can also lead to inflationary pressures, which we'll explore shortly. For investors with exposure to both capital markets and real estate, GDP provides a unifying metric for evaluating opportunities across asset classes.

Inflation: The Silent Force

Inflation reflects the rate at which prices for goods and services rise over time, eroding purchasing power.

While moderate inflation is a sign of healthy economic growth, excessive inflation can destabilise markets, while deflation (a decrease in prices) often signals economic distress.

Real estate is uniquely positioned in its relationship with inflation.

On one hand, inflation increases construction costs, which can drive up property values. On the other hand, real estate often serves as a hedge against inflation.

Rental income and property prices tend to rise in line with or above inflation, preserving real estate's value as an asset class.

For example, during periods of rising inflation, landlords may increase rents to match the higher costs of maintaining properties, ensuring that their investments remain profitable.

Similarly, investors in Real Estate Investment Trusts (REITs) often benefit from inflation-indexed leases, which pass inflationary pressures onto tenants.

From a capital markets perspective, inflation has far-reaching implications. Rising inflation often leads central banks to tighten monetary policy by raising interest rates, a topic we'll discuss in detail below.

For bond investors, inflation erodes the purchasing power of fixed-income payments, while equities may face pressure as higher costs squeeze corporate profits.

Understanding the interplay between inflation and real estate is crucial for capital markets professionals seeking to balance risk and reward.

Interest Rates: The Cost of Capital

Interest rates are perhaps the most directly impactful economic indicator for both capital markets and real estate.

As the cost of borrowing, interest rates influence everything from mortgage affordability to corporate financing decisions.

Central banks, such as the Federal Reserve or the European Central Bank, set benchmark interest rates to regulate economic activity, using them as a lever to combat inflation or stimulate growth.

In the real estate market, interest rates determine the cost of mortgages and loans. Low interest rates make borrowing more affordable, driving demand for residential and commercial properties. Developers benefit from reduced financing costs, enabling more projects to come to fruition.

However, rising interest rates can dampen demand, as higher borrowing costs deter buyers and increase the risk of default for existing loans.

For capital markets, interest rates shape the relative attractiveness of different asset classes. Rising rates can lead to higher bond yields, drawing capital away from equities and other riskier investments.

However, they can also create challenges for real estate-backed securities, such as mortgage-backed securities (MBS), as discussed in Chapter 7.

Investors must navigate these dynamics carefully, balancing the potential for higher returns against the risks of declining asset values.

The Interplay of Indicators

While each of these economic indicators, GDP, inflation, and interest rates, has a distinct impact, their interplay creates a complex web of influences that shape real estate and capital markets.

For example, during a period of GDP growth, rising incomes and consumer confidence may fuel demand for real estate. However, if growth leads to inflationary pressures, central banks may respond by raising interest rates. This, in turn, increases borrowing costs, potentially cooling the real estate market. For capital markets specialists, understanding these connections is key to making informed investment decisions that align with broader economic trends.

For real estate professionals, these dynamics underscore the importance of timing and strategy. Developing a project during a period of low interest rates can enhance profitability, but anticipating future rate hikes is critical for managing long-term costs. Similarly, understanding how GDP growth drives market demand can help developers position their projects to capture emerging opportunities.

Practical Examples

Consider the impact of these indicators during an economic expansion. Rising GDP might lead to increased demand for office space as businesses hire more workers. However, if inflation begins to rise alongside GDP, construction costs may increase, squeezing developers' profit margins. If central banks respond by raising interest rates, the cost of financing new projects may also rise, requiring developers to reassess their plans.

Alternatively, during an economic downturn, falling GDP may lead to reduced demand for retail and office spaces, while rising unemployment impacts residential markets. Inflation may slow, and central banks may lower interest rates to stimulate growth, creating opportunities for investors to acquire undervalued properties or refinance existing loans.

These examples illustrate the interconnectedness of economic indicators and their profound impact on real estate and capital markets. For professionals in both fields, staying attuned to these trends is essential for navigating challenges and seizing opportunities.

Building on Previous Insights

This chapter builds on the foundational concepts explored in earlier chapters.

From the financial ecosystem of real estate (Chapter 3) to the role of debt and equity financing (Chapters 4 and 5), economic indicators provide the context within which these mechanisms operate. The influence of GDP, inflation, and interest rates also ties into the themes of institutional capital (Chapter 6) and securitization (Chapter 7), highlighting the broader forces that shape market dynamics.

For readers who wish to explore these principles further, my previous book, *Real Estate Economics: Property, Markets, Principles, and Practices*, offers a deep dive into the economic theories that underpin real estate markets.

By combining the insights from that book with the practical applications discussed here, you can gain a comprehensive understanding of the economic drivers that influence your industry.

Looking Ahead

As we transition to the next chapter, the focus will shift to global trends in real estate capital markets.

We'll examine how cross-border investments and international economic conditions shape opportunities and challenges for both real estate and capital markets professionals. The economic indicators discussed here will continue to play a central role, providing the foundation for understanding these global dynamics.

Conclusion: Navigating Economic Forces

Economic indicators are the guiding stars of real estate and capital markets, providing critical insights into the forces that shape opportunities and risks. GDP, inflation, and interest rates each tell a part of the story, but their true significance lies in their interplay and impact on market dynamics.

For real estate professionals, understanding these indicators is key to planning projects, securing funding, and positioning assets for success. For capital markets specialists, they offer a lens through which to evaluate investment strategies and align portfolios with broader economic trends.

The journey continues, uncovering the connections and strategies that define success in this evolving ecosystem.

Let's move forward, building on the insights gained here to explore the global forces shaping the future of real estate and capital markets.

Chapter 10: Globalization of Real Estate

The globalization of real estate capital markets represents one of the most transformative trends in modern finance.

Over the past few decades, cross-border investments have surged, with capital flowing freely between countries, continents, and economies.

Once confined to local or national markets, real estate has evolved into a globally interconnected asset class.

Investors now pursue opportunities across borders, seeking higher returns, diversification, and exposure to emerging markets. Meanwhile, developers and property owners increasingly turn to international capital to fund projects.

Globalization offers vast opportunities but also introduces new complexities.

The interplay of foreign investment, local market dynamics, regulatory environments, and cultural nuances creates a multifaceted landscape that requires both strategic vision and deep expertise.

This chapter examines the rise of cross-border investments in real estate capital markets, their implications for stakeholders, and the trends shaping this global phenomenon.

Let's resume.

The Rise of Cross-Border Investments

The globalization of real estate capital markets began as an outgrowth of broader economic integration.

Advances in technology, communication, and transportation made it easier for investors to access opportunities beyond their borders. At the same time, the liberalization of trade and financial policies in many countries opened doors to foreign capital, fostering an environment of global connectivity.

Institutional investors, such as sovereign wealth funds, pension funds, and private equity firms, were among the first to embrace cross-border real estate investments. These entities sought to diversify their portfolios by investing in properties that offered stable returns in markets with favorable economic conditions. For example, a pension fund in North America might allocate capital to office developments in Europe, while an Asian sovereign wealth fund might invest in logistics hubs in the United States.

Cross-border investments are not limited to institutional players. High-net-worth individuals and family offices have also become active participants in the global real estate market. Many are drawn to international properties as a way to hedge against political or economic instability in their home countries. Luxury residential properties, commercial office buildings, and mixed-use developments are among the most popular asset classes for these investors.

The proliferation of Real Estate Investment Trusts (REITs) has further fueled cross-border investments. REITs allow investors to gain exposure to international real estate markets without directly owning properties, providing a liquid and transparent way to participate in global trends.

This democratization of real estate investment has made it possible for retail investors to diversify internationally, further amplifying the globalization of real estate capital markets.

Trends Driving Globalization

Several key trends are driving the globalization of real estate capital markets, reshaping the industry and creating new opportunities for stakeholders.

One of the most significant trends is the rise of emerging markets. Countries in Asia, Africa, and Latin America are experiencing rapid urbanization, population growth, and economic expansion, making them attractive destinations for real estate investment. Cities like Shanghai, São Paulo, and Lagos have become hubs for cross-border capital, offering high-growth opportunities for developers and investors alike.

Technological advancements are another driving force. Digital platforms, data analytics, and artificial intelligence have revolutionized how investors identify, evaluate, and manage global real estate opportunities. Technology enables real-time access to market data, streamlines due diligence processes, and facilitates cross-border transactions, breaking down barriers that once limited international investments.

Economic integration and trade agreements have also played a pivotal role. Regional alliances such as the European Union (EU), the North American Free Trade Agreement (NAFTA), and the Association of

Southeast Asian Nations (ASEAN) have created more accessible pathways for cross-border capital flows. These agreements reduce regulatory hurdles, harmonize legal frameworks, and encourage collaboration among member states, fostering a more connected global real estate market.

Finally, sustainability and environmental, social, and governance (ESG) considerations are reshaping the globalization of real estate. International investors are increasingly prioritizing green building certifications, energy efficiency, and social impact when evaluating properties.

This trend aligns with broader global efforts to combat climate change and promote sustainable development, influencing how and where capital is deployed.

Challenges and Risks

While globalization offers significant opportunities, it also introduces a range of challenges and risks that stakeholders must navigate.

One of the primary challenges is understanding and complying with local regulations and legal frameworks. Real estate laws vary widely between jurisdictions, covering everything from property ownership and taxation to zoning and environmental standards. For investors and developers operating across borders, navigating these legal complexities is critical to avoiding costly pitfalls and ensuring successful transactions.

This is where my previous book, *Real Estate Law Essentials: Navigate Transactions to Avoid Pitfalls and Seize Opportunities*, provides invaluable insights.

In the context of globalization, understanding real estate law is not just an advantage, it's a necessity. Whether you're evaluating opportunities in a new market or managing cross-border partnerships, a deep knowledge of legal principles can help you mitigate risks and capitalize on opportunities. For readers interested in exploring these topics further, I highly recommend delving into that book for a comprehensive guide to real estate law essentials.

Currency risk is another significant consideration in cross-border investments.

Exchange rate fluctuations can erode returns or increase costs, particularly in volatile or emerging markets. Investors often use hedging strategies to mitigate this risk, but these tools add complexity to the investment process.

Cultural differences and market nuances also pose challenges. Real estate is inherently local, shaped by cultural preferences, historical contexts, and social dynamics.

What works in one market may not translate to another, requiring investors and developers to adapt their strategies to align with local expectations.

Implications for Stakeholders

The globalization of real estate capital markets has profound implications for both real estate professionals and capital markets specialists.

For real estate professionals, globalization expands the pool of potential investors, creating new funding opportunities for projects of all sizes. Developers who can position their properties to appeal to international investors stand to benefit significantly from this trend. However, this requires a deep understanding of global market dynamics, cultural preferences, and regulatory requirements.

For capital markets specialists, the globalization of real estate presents an opportunity to diversify portfolios and access high-growth markets. Cross-border investments offer exposure to regions with different economic cycles, reducing overall portfolio risk. However, success in this arena requires a nuanced understanding of global trends, macroeconomic indicators, and the interplay between local and international forces.

Practical Examples

Consider the case of a logistics hub in Southeast Asia funded by North American and European investors.

The project is strategically located to capitalize on the region's booming e-commerce industry, which has driven demand for modern, efficient distribution centers. By pooling cross-border capital, the developers can deliver a state-of-the-art facility that meets global standards while addressing local market needs.

Another example is the acquisition of luxury residential properties in major global cities by high-net-worth individuals. These investments are often motivated by a combination of financial returns and lifestyle considerations, reflecting the unique intersection of personal and professional objectives in the global real estate market.

These examples illustrate how globalization enables collaboration, innovation, and value creation across borders, benefiting stakeholders in both real estate and capital markets.

Looking Ahead

As we move forward, the globalization of real estate capital markets will continue to evolve, shaped by technological advancements, economic shifts, and changing investor priorities.

Understanding the trends and challenges discussed in this chapter is essential for navigating this dynamic landscape.

In the next chapter, we'll explore how emerging technologies are transforming real estate and capital markets, creating new opportunities for innovation and disruption.

The globalization of these industries serves as a foundation for this transformation, connecting markets and stakeholders in unprecedented ways.

Conclusion: A Borderless Future

The globalization of real estate capital markets represents a new frontier for investors, developers, and financial professionals.

By enabling cross-border capital flows, fostering collaboration, and driving innovation, globalization has redefined what is possible in the real estate industry.

For real estate professionals, embracing globalization means accessing new funding sources, expanding market reach, and navigating diverse cultural and regulatory landscapes. For capital markets specialists, it offers opportunities to diversify portfolios, enhance returns, and contribute to the development of global communities.

As we continue this journey, remember that understanding the intricacies of globalization requires both strategic vision and detailed knowledge. By building on the insights gained here, you can position yourself to thrive in this interconnected world of real estate and capital markets.

Chapter 11: Risk Management

Risk is an inherent part of any investment, and the intersection of real estate and capital markets is no exception. As we've explored in earlier chapters, the globalization of real estate capital markets (Chapter 10) and the foundational principles of these interconnected markets (Chapter 1) have created immense opportunities but also introduced significant challenges. To thrive in this dynamic landscape, both real estate professionals and capital markets specialists must adopt a proactive and comprehensive approach to risk management.

This chapter delves into the common risks faced by stakeholders in real estate capital markets, exploring their causes, implications, and strategies for mitigation. By viewing real estate capital markets as a unified entity, we aim to provide readers with a cohesive understanding of how risks arise and how they can be managed effectively.

Let's continue.

Understanding Risk in Real Estate Capital Markets

Risk in real estate capital markets can be broadly categorized into market risks, operational risks, and systemic risks.

These categories overlap and interact in complex ways, reflecting the multifaceted nature of the industry.

Market risks stem from fluctuations in economic indicators, such as GDP, inflation, and interest rates (as discussed in Chapters 1 and 9).

These factors influence property values, rental income, and the performance of real estate-backed securities, creating volatility for investors and developers.

Operational risks arise from the day-to-day management of real estate assets and transactions.

These risks include tenant defaults, maintenance issues, and legal disputes, all of which can disrupt cash flows and erode asset value.

Systemic risks are tied to broader economic and financial systems, encompassing events such as market crashes, geopolitical tensions, and regulatory changes.

These risks can have far-reaching consequences, affecting multiple stakeholders and markets simultaneously.

By understanding these categories and their interconnections, stakeholders can develop strategies to identify, assess, and mitigate risks, ensuring resilience and stability in their investments.

Common Risks in Real Estate Capital Markets

Economic Volatility is one of the most significant risks in real estate capital markets.

Changes in GDP growth, inflation, and interest rates can have cascading effects on property values, financing costs, and investor sentiment. For example, a sudden economic downturn may lead to decreased demand for commercial properties, rising vacancy rates, and declining rental income.

Currency risk is another critical concern in the globalized real estate capital markets. For investors engaging in cross-border transactions, fluctuations in exchange rates can significantly impact returns. For instance, a depreciation of the local currency relative to the investor's home currency may erode the value of rental income and capital gains.

Regulatory risk arises from changes in laws and policies that affect real estate transactions, financing, and ownership. For example, new zoning regulations, tax policies, or foreign investment restrictions can disrupt projects and alter market dynamics. As highlighted in Chapter 10, understanding local legal frameworks is essential for navigating these risks, and readers are again encouraged to consult my book *Real Estate Law Essentials* for a deeper dive into this topic.

Liquidity risk is a perennial challenge in real estate capital markets. While public markets offer liquidity through tradable securities like REITs, private real estate investments are often illiquid, requiring significant time and effort to sell. During periods of market stress, this lack of liquidity can amplify losses and limit strategic flexibility.

Tenant risk is particularly relevant for income-generating properties, such as commercial and residential rentals. Tenant defaults, lease terminations, or difficulties in securing new tenants can disrupt cash flows and reduce asset value. This risk is compounded during economic downturns when businesses and households face financial pressures.

Geopolitical risk reflects the interconnectedness of global markets and the vulnerability of real estate capital markets to international events. Trade disputes, political instability, or conflicts can create uncertainty, disrupt cross-border investments, and alter market conditions.

Strategies for Risk Mitigation

Risk management in real estate capital markets requires a holistic and proactive approach, combining financial, operational, and strategic measures.

Diversification is one of the most effective strategies for mitigating risk. By spreading investments across different asset classes, geographies, and sectors, stakeholders can reduce their exposure to specific risks.

For example, an investor might allocate capital to a mix of residential, commercial, and industrial properties across multiple countries, balancing high-growth opportunities with stable, income-generating assets.

Hedging is a critical tool for managing currency and interest rate risks. For cross-border investments, currency hedging instruments, such as forward contracts or options, can protect against exchange rate fluctuations.

Similarly, interest rate swaps or caps can shield borrowers from rising financing costs, ensuring predictability in cash flows.

Due diligence is a cornerstone of risk management, providing stakeholders with the information needed to make informed decisions. This includes thorough market analysis, property inspections, financial assessments, and legal reviews. As discussed in Chapter 10, understanding local regulations and cultural nuances is essential for navigating the complexities of global real estate capital markets.

Active asset management is key to mitigating operational risks.

This involves maintaining properties to high standards, ensuring tenant satisfaction, and addressing issues promptly.

For income-generating assets, robust lease agreements and tenant screening processes can reduce the likelihood of defaults and disputes.

Scenario planning allows stakeholders to anticipate and prepare for potential risks. By modeling different scenarios, such as economic recessions or regulatory changes, investors and developers can identify vulnerabilities and develop contingency plans.

This approach fosters resilience and adaptability in the face of uncertainty.

Insurance is another vital component of risk management, providing financial protection against unforeseen events.

From property insurance to liability coverage, a well-structured insurance program can mitigate the impact of natural disasters, accidents, or legal claims.

Collaborative partnerships can also enhance risk management.

By working with experienced professionals, such as property managers, legal advisors, and financial consultants, stakeholders can leverage expertise and resources to address challenges effectively.

The Interplay of Risk and Opportunity

While risk is often perceived as a threat, it also creates opportunities for innovation and growth. For example, market volatility may present opportunities to acquire undervalued assets, while regulatory changes may create incentives for sustainable development.

The globalization of real estate capital markets, as discussed in Chapter 10, has amplified both risks and opportunities, requiring stakeholders to adopt a global perspective in their risk management strategies.

By understanding the interconnectedness of markets and the forces that drive them, stakeholders can position themselves to capitalize on emerging trends while mitigating potential threats.

Practical Examples

Consider the case of a global real estate investment fund managing a diversified portfolio of properties across North America, Europe, and Asia. To mitigate currency risk, the fund employs hedging strategies, using forward contracts to lock in exchange rates for anticipated cash flows. At the same time, the fund conducts scenario planning to assess the potential impact of geopolitical tensions on its assets, identifying vulnerabilities and adjusting its strategy accordingly.

Another example is a commercial property developer navigating regulatory changes in a major metropolitan area. By conducting thorough due diligence and engaging with local authorities, the developer ensures compliance with new zoning laws, avoiding delays and penalties. The developer also collaborates with legal advisors to structure agreements that protect against tenant risks, ensuring stable cash flows for the property.

These examples illustrate the importance of a proactive and comprehensive approach to risk management, combining financial, operational, and strategic measures to navigate the complexities of real estate capital markets.

Referencing the Foundation

As we consider risk management, it's essential to revisit the foundational principles discussed in earlier chapters. Chapter 1 introduced the interconnectedness of real estate and capital markets, setting the stage for understanding how risks arise in this unified ecosystem.

Chapter 10 explored the globalization of these markets, highlighting the opportunities and challenges of cross-border investments.

Together, these chapters provide the context for understanding the dynamics of risk and the strategies needed to manage it effectively.

Looking Ahead

As we move into the next chapter, we'll explore innovative approaches to financing in real estate capital markets, examining how new technologies and financial instruments are transforming the industry. Risk management will remain a central theme, influencing how stakeholders navigate these innovations and their implications.

Conclusion: Navigating the Risks

Risk is an inevitable aspect of real estate capital markets, reflecting the complexity and dynamism of these interconnected industries.

By understanding the common risks and adopting proactive strategies for mitigation, stakeholders can navigate challenges and seize opportunities with confidence.

For real estate professionals, risk management involves balancing operational excellence with strategic foresight, ensuring the stability and growth of assets. For capital markets specialists, it requires a nuanced understanding of market dynamics, financial instruments, and global trends.

As we continue this journey, remember that risk is not merely a threat but a driver of innovation and progress. By embracing a comprehensive approach to risk management, you can thrive in the evolving world of real estate capital markets, building resilience and unlocking new possibilities.

Chapter 12: Alternative Investments

The landscape of real estate capital markets is undergoing a seismic shift.

Traditional methods of investing, while foundational, are increasingly being supplemented by innovative and alternative opportunities that cater to the demands of modern investors.

From crowdfunding platforms to renewable energy projects, alternative investments are redefining the way real estate and capital markets operate as a unified ecosystem.

In this chapter, we refine the discussion on alternative investment opportunities, providing sharper examples, reducing redundancy, and enhancing clarity.

These opportunities not only highlight the dynamic nature of real estate capital markets but also reflect the increasing interplay of innovation, linked markets, and strategic diversification.

For further insights into structuring these investments, my book *Raising Money for Real*

Estate Investments: Close Deals, Raise Money, Build Wealth remains an essential guide.

Let's continue.

The Nature of Alternatives in Real Estate

Alternative investments within real estate capital markets go beyond conventional asset classes, such as residential homes or commercial office buildings. These opportunities span niche markets and innovative sectors that offer distinct benefits, including higher returns, diversification, and access to emerging industries.

Unlike traditional investments, alternatives often involve non-traditional financing methods, new technologies, or untapped markets. For example, industrial properties linked to e-commerce logistics, or green infrastructure projects focused on sustainability, are redefining the boundaries of what constitutes real estate investment.

Such alternatives are gaining traction among real estate professionals seeking unique funding solutions and among capital markets participants eager to integrate tangible assets with innovative strategies. These opportunities are characterized by their adaptability, resilience, and alignment with global trends, making them invaluable in today's complex financial landscape.

Emerging Trends in Alternative Real Estate Markets

The rapid rise of crowdfunding platforms is democratizing real estate investments.

These platforms allow developers to pool resources from individual investors, each contributing relatively small amounts of capital. Crowdfunding facilitates the funding of boutique projects, such as co-living spaces or eco-friendly developments, which may not appeal to traditional institutional investors.

Another transformative trend is the application of blockchain technology in real estate transactions. Blockchain enables the creation of tokenized real estate assets, allowing investors to buy fractional ownership in properties. This innovation reduces entry barriers, enhances liquidity, and provides unparalleled transparency. Blockchain's ability to streamline cross-border transactions has been particularly impactful, echoing themes from Chapter 10 on globalization.

The sustainability movement has also fueled interest in alternative real estate investments. Green buildings and renewable energy projects, such as solar farms integrated into real estate developments, are increasingly sought after for their dual promise of financial returns and environmental impact. These projects align with the broader push for Environmental, Social, and Governance (ESG) compliance, making them attractive to a wide range of investors.

Specialized real estate funds are another noteworthy trend. These funds focus on alternative assets, such as healthcare facilities, student housing, or data centers, leveraging deep expertise to maximize returns.

Their tailored strategies appeal to investors seeking targeted exposure to high-growth sectors.

Linked Markets and Strategic Diversification

Alternative investments are uniquely positioned to bridge real estate capital markets with other linked sectors, creating opportunities for diversification and synergy.

For example, the logistics sector has seen explosive growth due to the rise of e-commerce, driving demand for strategically located distribution centers.

Investors in logistics hubs benefit not only from property appreciation but also from their connection to global trade networks.

Similarly, the renewable energy sector has emerged as a key area of overlap.

Real estate projects incorporating solar installations or wind turbines offer steady income streams from energy generation, complemented by the long-term stability of property investments.

For investors, these dual-purpose assets provide a hedge against traditional market volatility.

Healthcare is another linked market with significant potential.

From senior living facilities to outpatient clinics, healthcare real estate combines stable demand with resilience to economic fluctuations.

As populations age and healthcare delivery evolves, this sector offers both financial security and societal impact.

These linked markets not only enhance portfolio diversification but also demonstrate the adaptability of real estate capital markets to align with global trends and emerging opportunities.

Structuring Alternative Investments: Lessons from *Raising Money for Real Estate Investments*

Structuring alternative investments requires a deep understanding of investor needs, project dynamics, and market trends.

My book, *Raising Money for Real Estate Investments: Close Deals, Raise Money, Build Wealth*, provides practical guidance on structuring deals that attract funding while aligning with strategic goals.

Joint ventures are a versatile structure for alternative investments. By partnering with specialized firms or institutional investors, developers can share risks and leverage expertise. For example, a joint venture might pair a real estate developer with a renewable energy company to create a hybrid project integrating solar panels with residential housing.

Crowdfunding platforms, as discussed earlier, offer another innovative structure. These platforms enable developers to access a wide pool of investors, reducing dependency on traditional financing methods. Crowdfunding is particularly effective for smaller projects targeting specific niches, such as co-working spaces tailored for creative industries.

Private equity funds also play a pivotal role in alternative investments. These funds pool resources to target high-growth opportunities in sectors like data centers or student housing. By focusing on value-add strategies, private equity funds create opportunities for significant returns, albeit with higher associated risks.

These structures illustrate the importance of flexibility and creativity in raising money for alternative investments.

By tailoring approaches to specific projects and investor profiles, stakeholders can unlock the full potential of these opportunities.

Examples of Alternative Opportunities

Consider the development of a state-of-the-art data center in a major metropolitan area.

These facilities, essential for supporting cloud computing and online services, attract long-term leases from technology companies.

By integrating green energy solutions, such as solar power, the developer not only reduces operational costs but also aligns with ESG priorities, enhancing the project's appeal to institutional investors.

Another example is the conversion of underutilized urban office spaces into mixed-use developments incorporating co-living units and shared workspaces. These projects cater to the growing demand for flexible living and working arrangements, particularly among younger demographics.

Crowdfunding platforms often play a key role in financing such initiatives, enabling communities to participate in revitalizing their neighborhoods.

A third example involves investing in healthcare facilities, such as outpatient clinics or senior housing. These properties benefit from stable demand and government incentives, making them attractive to both private equity funds and individual investors.

By structuring these investments with long-term leases and inflation-adjusted rents, stakeholders can ensure predictable income streams.

These examples underscore the adaptability and innovation inherent in alternative real estate investments, highlighting their potential to address diverse market needs while delivering strong financial performance.

Risks and Considerations

While alternative investments offer significant opportunities, they also present unique challenges that require careful navigation.

One of the most pressing risks is market uncertainty.

Sectors like blockchain-enabled real estate or renewable energy are still evolving, creating potential for rapid changes in demand, technology, or regulation. Investors must remain vigilant and adaptable to stay ahead of these shifts.

Regulatory challenges are another critical consideration. Many alternative investments operate in uncharted territory, with limited regulatory oversight.

Understanding the legal frameworks governing these markets is essential, as compliance failures can result in financial losses or reputational damage.

Liquidity constraints also pose challenges. Niche assets, such as data centers or green infrastructure projects, may lack a broad buyer pool, making them difficult to sell quickly.

This illiquidity must be balanced against the potential for higher returns.

Operational complexities are a further consideration. Managing alternative assets often requires specialized knowledge and resources, whether it's ensuring tenant satisfaction in co-living spaces or optimizing energy output from renewable installations.

Partnering with experienced operators can help mitigate these risks and enhance asset performance.

Looking Ahead

The alternative investment landscape within real estate capital markets is poised for continued growth, driven by innovation, global trends, and evolving investor preferences.

These opportunities offer a pathway to diversification, higher returns, and alignment with societal priorities, such as sustainability and technological advancement.

In the next chapter, we will explore how technology continues to transform real estate capital markets, examining the tools and platforms reshaping the industry.

Alternative investments will remain a central theme, reflecting the broader shift toward innovation and adaptability in this dynamic ecosystem.

Conclusion: Unlocking New Possibilities

Alternative investments represent the forefront of real estate capital markets, offering a diverse array of opportunities that challenge conventional approaches. For real estate professionals, these investments provide avenues to address emerging market needs and expand project portfolios. For capital markets specialists, they offer innovative ways to align investments with global trends and niche opportunities.

By leveraging the insights and strategies discussed here, as well as the practical guidance provided in *Raising Money for Real Estate Investments*, stakeholders can position themselves to thrive in this evolving landscape.

The future of real estate capital markets lies in adaptability, creativity, and a willingness to explore the unconventional.

Chapter 13: ESG and Sustainable Investing

In an era of climate change, social accountability, and governance transparency, Environmental, Social, and Governance (ESG) factors have emerged as critical considerations.

This applies to all investors, developers, and stakeholders in real estate capital markets.

ESG principles are no longer optional; they are essential for aligning investment strategies with global priorities, mitigating risks, and creating long-term value.

While we touched on ESG briefly in Chapter 12, this chapter delves deeply into its significance. It will explore the drivers, benefits, challenges, and effectiveness of ESG-focused investing in real estate.

The importance of ESG lies not only in its moral and societal implications but also in its ability to enhance financial performance and mitigate risks.

Let's continue.

The Foundations of ESG

ESG (Environmental, Social, and Governance) represents three essential dimensions shaping modern investment decisions and real estate practices.

Environmental factors focus on sustainability and energy efficiency, including waste management, reducing carbon footprints, and integrating green building practices into real estate projects. These considerations are increasingly important as investors and developers address climate change and resource efficiency.

Social factors emphasize the human side of real estate, such as fostering community engagement, ensuring tenant satisfaction, and promoting equitable development that benefits diverse stakeholders.

Governance factors highlight the importance of transparency, ethical practices, and accountability in property management and investment strategies. Together, ESG principles provide a comprehensive framework for aligning real estate projects with both financial objectives and broader societal goals.

Together, these pillars form a framework that allows investors to assess the broader impact of their investments beyond traditional financial metrics.

ESG considerations enable stakeholders to identify risks and opportunities that may not be immediately apparent in conventional analyses, creating a more holistic approach to decision-making.

In real estate, ESG principles are particularly relevant due to the sector's significant environmental impact, social role, and governance complexities. Buildings account for nearly 40% of global carbon emissions, making the industry a key target for sustainability initiatives.

At the same time, real estate developments shape communities, influence social outcomes, and require robust governance structures to ensure ethical practices.

The Rise of ESG in Real Estate

The adoption of ESG principles in real estate has been driven by several factors, including regulatory pressures, investor demand, and shifting societal priorities.

Regulatory frameworks at local, national, and international levels are increasingly mandating sustainable practices in construction, energy use, and waste management.

For example, many governments offer incentives for green building certifications or impose penalties for failing to meet energy efficiency standards.

These regulations create a strong incentive for developers and investors to incorporate ESG principles into their projects.

Investor demand has also played a pivotal role. Institutional investors, including pension funds and sovereign wealth funds, are prioritizing ESG-aligned assets as part of their long-term strategies.

These investors recognize that properties with strong ESG credentials are more resilient to risks, such as regulatory changes or climate-related disruptions, and are likely to deliver stable returns.

Societal priorities have further accelerated the ESG movement. Consumers, tenants, and employees are increasingly favoring companies and properties that align with their values, driving demand for sustainable and socially responsible real estate.

From co-living spaces designed with inclusivity in mind to office buildings with high energy performance ratings, ESG considerations are shaping market preferences.

Environmental Factors: Sustainability in Focus

The environmental pillar of ESG is perhaps the most visible in real estate, reflecting the industry's significant impact on energy use, emissions, and resource consumption.

Sustainable real estate practices aim to minimize this impact while maximizing efficiency and resilience.

Green building certifications, such as LEED (Leadership in Energy and Environmental Design) or BREEAM (Building Research Establishment Environmental Assessment Method), have become benchmarks for sustainability in real estate.

These certifications assess properties based on criteria such as energy efficiency, water conservation, and waste reduction, providing a tangible measure of environmental performance.

Energy efficiency is a critical component of ESG-aligned real estate. Properties equipped with solar panels, energy-efficient HVAC systems, and smart building technologies not only reduce emissions but also lower operating costs, enhancing their appeal to tenants and investors.

Climate resilience is another key consideration.

Properties located in areas prone to flooding, hurricanes, or wildfires face significant risks, both in terms of physical damage and insurance costs. ESG-aligned investments prioritize resilience measures, such as elevated construction, green roofs, or stormwater management systems, to mitigate these risks.

Social Factors: The Human Element

The social pillar of ESG focuses on the impact of real estate on people and communities.

This dimension emphasizes inclusivity, equity, and well-being, addressing the social challenges associated with urbanization and development.

Community engagement is a cornerstone of socially responsible real estate. Developers who involve local stakeholders in planning processes can create projects that align with community needs, fostering goodwill and reducing resistance.

For example, mixed-use developments that incorporate affordable housing, public spaces, and community services can enhance social outcomes while delivering financial returns.

Tenant satisfaction is another critical factor. Properties that prioritize tenant well-being, such as through access to green spaces, high-quality amenities, or flexible lease terms, are more likely to retain occupants and maintain stable cash flows.

Socially responsible property management practices, such as equitable rent policies or support for small businesses, further enhance tenant relationships.

Equitable development is particularly relevant in addressing issues of gentrification and displacement.

ESG-aligned investments strive to balance economic growth with social equity, ensuring that development benefits all members of a community rather than exacerbating inequalities.

Governance Factors: Accountability and Transparency

The governance pillar of ESG focuses on the systems and processes that ensure ethical practices, accountability, and transparency in real estate investments.

Effective governance is essential for building trust among stakeholders and mitigating risks associated with mismanagement or fraud.

Transparency is a fundamental aspect of governance. Investors and tenants increasingly demand clear and accessible information about a property's performance, sustainability initiatives, and management practices.

ESG-aligned real estate projects prioritize transparency by providing detailed reporting and open communication.

Ethical practices are another key consideration. From fair labor standards in construction to anti-corruption policies in property management, governance frameworks ensure that real estate investments align with ethical principles.

These practices not only enhance reputation but also reduce legal and reputational risks.

Diversity and inclusion in leadership are also gaining prominence.

ESG-aligned organizations recognize that diverse leadership teams are better equipped to address complex challenges and foster innovation, making diversity a strategic priority.

Pros and Cons of ESG in Real Estate

While ESG principles bring significant advantages to real estate and investment, they also present challenges that stakeholders must address.

On the positive side, ESG-aligned properties demonstrate greater resilience to regulatory changes, climate risks, and market disruptions, thereby enhancing their long-term value. Sustainable practices, such as energy-efficient designs and waste reduction, not only lower operating costs but also improve tenant satisfaction, contributing to more stable cash flows.

Moreover, ESG compliance often attracts institutional investors and tenants who prioritise sustainability and social responsibility, making such properties more competitive in the market.

However, adopting ESG initiatives is not without its hurdles. Implementing sustainable measures often entails higher upfront costs, such as expenses for green certifications or renewable energy systems, which can deter some stakeholders.

Additionally, measuring and reporting ESG performance can be complex and resource-intensive, posing challenges, particularly for smaller organisations with limited resources. Balancing social and environmental goals with financial objectives can also prove difficult, requiring trade-offs and careful prioritisation to achieve meaningful and sustainable outcomes.

These pros and cons underscore the need for strategic planning and commitment to fully realise the potential of ESG integration in real estate.

Despite these challenges, the effectiveness of ESG in real estate is increasingly evident.

Studies show that ESG-aligned assets tend to outperform their peers over the long term, both financially and in terms of resilience.

Effectiveness of ESG: Real-World Examples

Consider the case of a green-certified office building in a major urban center. By incorporating solar panels, energy-efficient lighting, and a rainwater harvesting system, the building reduces its carbon footprint while lowering operating costs. These features not only attract tenants seeking sustainable spaces but also enhance the property's appeal to investors focused on ESG compliance.

Another example is a mixed-use development that integrates affordable housing, public transportation access, and community spaces. This project balances financial returns with social impact, creating a vibrant community while addressing housing affordability challenges.

A third example involves a real estate investment trust (REIT) that prioritizes transparency and ethical practices. By providing detailed ESG reporting and adopting diversity initiatives, the REIT builds trust with investors and tenants, strengthening its market position.

Looking Ahead

As ESG continues to gain prominence, its influence on real estate capital markets will only grow.

Stakeholders who embrace ESG principles will be better positioned to navigate regulatory changes, attract investment, and meet the demands of an evolving market.

In the next chapter, we will explore the role of technology in advancing ESG initiatives, examining how digital tools and data analytics are transforming sustainable investing in real estate capital markets.

Conclusion: A Framework for the Future

ESG represents a fundamental shift in how real estate and capital markets approach investment, emphasizing sustainability, social responsibility, and governance.

For stakeholders, adopting ESG principles is not just a matter of compliance, it is a pathway to creating long-term value and addressing global challenges.

By understanding the reasoning behind ESG and implementing its principles effectively, real estate professionals and capital markets specialists can drive positive change while achieving their financial goals.

The journey continues, uncovering the strategies and innovations that define the future of real estate capital markets.

Chapter 14: Future of Real Estate Markets

The intersection of technology and real estate capital markets is driving transformative changes that are redefining how assets are traded, managed, and valued.

Over the past decade, technological advancements have introduced new tools, platforms, and concepts that are reshaping traditional practices.

From blockchain's promise of transparency to the rise of PropTech and the revolutionary concept of tokenization, the future of real estate capital markets is undeniably digital.

This chapter offers a deep dive into the role of these technologies in shaping the future of real estate capital markets.

By the end, readers will have a clear understanding of these innovations, their potential, and the challenges they pose.

Let's learn more.

The Role of Technology in Real Estate Capital Markets

Technology has become a central force in real estate capital markets, bridging the gap between physical assets and digital ecosystems.

At its core, technology offers solutions to longstanding inefficiencies, enhancing transparency, accessibility, and operational efficiency.

Historically, real estate transactions have been time-consuming, opaque, and reliant on intermediaries.

Capital markets, while more liquid, often struggle with integrating real estate into their frameworks due to the sector's illiquidity and complexity.

Technology is addressing these challenges by creating tools that streamline processes, increase data transparency, and enable real-time decision-making.

For example, digital platforms now allow investors to evaluate properties, track market trends, and execute transactions remotely.

These platforms are particularly useful for cross-border investments, as discussed in Chapter 10, where technology reduces barriers such as language, legal complexities, and geographical distance.

As we delve deeper, we'll explore three key technologies that are shaping the future: blockchain, PropTech, and tokenization.

Blockchain: The Backbone of Transparent Transactions

Blockchain technology, best known as the foundation of cryptocurrencies, has found a natural home in real estate capital markets. At its core, blockchain is a decentralized digital ledger that records transactions across multiple systems, ensuring security, transparency, and immutability.

How Blockchain Works in Real Estate

In real estate, blockchain can revolutionize how properties are bought, sold, and managed. By creating a transparent and tamper-proof record of transactions, blockchain eliminates the need for intermediaries such as brokers, escrow agents, and title companies. This reduces transaction costs and speeds up processes, making real estate investments more accessible.

For example, when a property is sold, the transaction can be recorded on a blockchain, creating a permanent digital record that includes details such as ownership history, property condition, and financial transactions. This information is accessible to all parties, reducing disputes and ensuring trust.

Use Cases of Blockchain in Real Estate

Blockchain technology is transforming real estate through innovative applications such as smart contracts, tokenization, and title management. Smart contracts are self-executing agreements that automatically enforce the terms of a contract once specific conditions are met.

This technology streamlines processes like lease agreements, purchase transactions, and property management, ensuring compliance without the need for manual oversight. By reducing human error and administrative delays, smart contracts enhance efficiency and reliability in real estate operations.

Tokenization introduces a revolutionary way to trade real estate assets by creating digital tokens that represent ownership shares in properties. These tokens enable fractional ownership, allowing investors to buy and sell shares with unprecedented ease on digital platforms. This democratizes access to real estate investment and increases liquidity in the market.

Title management is another game-changing application, leveraging blockchain to store property titles securely and create a tamper-proof system for tracking ownership. By reducing fraud and simplifying title searches, especially in regions with weak registration systems, blockchain provides a transparent and efficient solution to traditional challenges in property ownership.

These advancements highlight the transformative potential of blockchain in modernizing real estate practices.

Benefits of Blockchain

- Transparency: Blockchain creates a clear and accessible record of transactions, reducing the risk of fraud or misinformation.
- Efficiency: By automating processes and eliminating intermediaries, blockchain reduces transaction costs and speeds up real estate deals.
- Global Access: Blockchain facilitates cross-border investments by standardizing transactions and removing the need for local intermediaries.

PropTech and Property Management

PropTech, short for property technology, refers to the application of technology to improve the buying, selling, and managing of real estate. From digital platforms that connect buyers with sellers to AI-powered tools that optimize property management, PropTech is transforming the industry at every level.

Key Areas of PropTech

1. Property Management Software: Modern property management platforms use AI and data analytics to streamline operations, from tenant communication to maintenance scheduling. These tools enable landlords and property managers to reduce costs, improve tenant satisfaction, and maximize returns.
2. Market Analytics: Platforms like Zillow or Redfin use big data to provide real-time market insights, helping investors identify trends and make informed decisions. These tools are particularly valuable in volatile markets, where data-driven strategies can mitigate risks.
3. Virtual and Augmented Reality (VR/AR): VR and AR technologies are revolutionizing property tours and marketing. Potential buyers or tenants can explore properties

remotely, saving time and resources while providing a more immersive experience.
4. **Sustainable Building Technologies:** PropTech also includes tools that enhance sustainability, such as energy monitoring systems, smart thermostats, and green building certifications. These technologies align with ESG principles, as discussed in Chapter 13, and are increasingly in demand among investors and tenants.

The Impact of PropTech on Real Estate Capital Markets

PropTech is not just a tool for improving operations; it is also a driver of innovation in capital markets. By providing investors with real-time data, automated reporting, and predictive analytics. For example, REITs can use PropTech to monitor portfolio performance and identify opportunities for optimization, ensuring better returns for shareholders.

Tokenization: The Future of Real Estate Investment

Tokenization represents one of the most exciting innovations in real estate capital markets. By converting real estate assets into digital tokens, this technology enables fractional ownership and creates a more liquid and accessible market.

How Tokenization Works

Tokenization involves creating digital tokens on a blockchain that represent ownership shares in a property. These tokens can be traded on digital platforms, allowing investors to buy and sell shares in real estate much like they would trade stocks or bonds.

For example, a commercial property worth $10 million could be divided into 10,000 tokens, each representing a $1,000 share. Investors can purchase tokens based on their budget, gaining exposure to high-value properties without the need for large capital outlays.

Benefits of Tokenization

- Accessibility: Tokenization lowers the barriers to entry for real estate investments, enabling smaller investors to participate in high-value projects.
- Liquidity: Tokens can be traded on digital platforms, providing investors with the flexibility to buy or sell their shares at any time.
- Diversification: By investing in tokens across multiple properties, investors can create a diversified portfolio with minimal effort.

Challenges of Tokenization

While tokenization offers significant benefits, it also presents challenges that must be addressed:

- Regulation: The regulatory environment for tokenized assets is still evolving, creating uncertainty for investors and issuers.
- Adoption: Tokenization requires widespread adoption by investors, developers, and financial institutions to achieve its full potential.
- Technology Risks: As a digital innovation, tokenization is vulnerable to cybersecurity threats and technological failures.

The Future of Real Estate Capital Markets

The integration of blockchain, PropTech, and tokenization is reshaping real estate capital markets, creating a future defined by transparency, efficiency, and accessibility.

However, the adoption of these technologies is not without challenges. Stakeholders must navigate regulatory uncertainties, technological complexities, and market resistance to fully realize their potential.

Looking ahead, the success of these innovations will depend on collaboration between real estate professionals, capital markets specialists, and technology providers.

By working together, these stakeholders can create a more dynamic, resilient, and inclusive market that benefits all participants.

Conclusion: Embracing Innovation

The future of real estate capital markets is being written by the transformative power of technology.

From blockchain's promise of transparency to the efficiency of PropTech and the accessibility of tokenization, these innovations are redefining how assets are managed, traded, and valued.

For real estate professionals, embracing these technologies offers a pathway to enhanced efficiency, sustainability, and profitability. For capital markets specialists, they provide tools to integrate real estate into diversified portfolios with greater ease and precision.

As we move forward, the ability to adapt to and leverage these technologies will be the defining factor for success in the evolving world of real estate capital markets.

By understanding the concepts and principles outlined in this chapter, stakeholders can position themselves to thrive in this exciting new era.

Chapter 15: Case Studies

The relationship between capital markets and real estate is best understood through the lens of real-world projects.

These examples highlight how the two sectors interlink, offering valuable lessons for professionals navigating this dynamic space.

Through case studies, we can explore the strategies, challenges, and outcomes of initiatives that bridge real estate and capital markets, revealing the intricate mechanics of their collaboration. This chapter examines fictionalized yet plausible examples of how capital markets and real estate converge.

Each case study sheds light on a different aspect of their interaction. By understanding these scenarios, readers can gain insights into the practical application of theories and strategies discussed in earlier chapters.

Let's start exploring case studies.

Case Study 1: Revitalizing Urban Cores

An urban redevelopment project was launched to transform a neglected city center into a vibrant mixed-use district. Capital markets played a pivotal role by providing funding through the issuance of municipal bonds, attracting institutional investors seeking stable returns. The project's real estate components included residential units, office spaces, and retail outlets designed to cater to a diverse urban population.

During the project's planning phase, market analysis indicated that revitalization would increase property values and stimulate local economic growth. Capital markets specialists structured the bond offering to include tax incentives, making it more attractive to investors. The collaboration between real estate developers and financial institutions ensured that funding was allocated efficiently, addressing both immediate construction needs and long-term maintenance.

The project's success underscored the importance of aligning public and private interests, demonstrating how real estate developments could leverage capital markets for urban transformation.

Case Study 2: Expanding Affordable Housing

A real estate investment trust (REIT) focused on affordable housing sought to address the growing demand for low-cost residential units in suburban areas.

The REIT raised capital through an initial public offering, allowing retail investors to participate in its mission-driven projects.

To maximize impact, the REIT partnered with local governments to secure land at reduced costs and implemented energy-efficient designs to lower operating expenses. Capital markets expertise was essential in structuring the offering to appeal to ESG-focused investors, aligning with principles of environmental sustainability and social equity.

The project demonstrated how capital markets could support socially responsible real estate initiatives while delivering competitive returns.

By integrating real estate strategies with financial instruments, the REIT successfully balanced profitability with community impact.

Case Study 3: Logistics Hub Development

A logistics hub project was initiated to support the region's booming e-commerce industry.

Real estate developers partnered with private equity firms to secure funding, leveraging the hub's strategic location near major highways and airports.

Capital markets played a crucial role in structuring the investment, with private equity firms pooling resources from institutional investors seeking exposure to industrial real estate.

The hub was designed with state-of-the-art facilities, including automated warehousing and sustainable energy solutions, to attract high-profile tenants.

The project highlighted the importance of aligning real estate development with emerging market trends.

By incorporating advanced logistics technology, the hub became a critical node in the global supply chain, offering both economic value and resilience.

Case Study 4: Green Office Tower

A green-certified office tower was developed in a major metropolitan area, targeting corporations seeking sustainable workspaces.

The project was financed through green bonds, a financial instrument designed to fund environmentally friendly initiatives.

Real estate developers collaborated with capital markets specialists to structure the bond issuance, ensuring compliance with international green standards.

The building incorporated renewable energy sources, water conservation systems, and smart technologies to enhance efficiency.

The success of the project demonstrated the potential of green bonds to align financial goals with sustainability objectives.

By integrating ESG principles into both the real estate and capital markets aspects, the office tower set a benchmark for future developments.

Case Study 5: Cross-Border Retail Investment

A cross-border retail investment project sought to develop shopping centers in emerging markets.

Real estate developers partnered with a global investment fund, leveraging the fund's expertise in navigating international markets.

Capital markets were instrumental in structuring the funding, with the investment fund raising capital through a combination of equity and debt instruments.

Real estate professionals conducted market research to identify high-growth regions and tailored the shopping centers to local preferences.

The project highlighted the challenges and opportunities of cross-border investments, emphasizing the importance of cultural sensitivity and regulatory compliance.

By aligning real estate strategies with global capital markets, the project achieved financial success while fostering economic development in underserved regions.

Case Study 6: Residential Tokenization

A residential property developer experimented with tokenization to democratize access to high-value real estate.

The project involved converting a luxury apartment complex into digital tokens, allowing investors to purchase fractional ownership through a blockchain platform.

Capital markets expertise was essential in structuring the token offering, ensuring regulatory compliance and investor protection.

The developer leveraged blockchain technology to enhance transparency, reduce transaction costs, and increase liquidity.

The project demonstrated the potential of tokenization to revolutionize real estate investment, offering a glimpse into the future of capital markets integration.

By embracing innovative technologies, the developer attracted a diverse pool of investors and expanded access to premium properties.

Case Study 7: Industrial Park Expansion

An industrial park expansion project was launched to meet the growing demand for manufacturing and storage facilities.

The project was funded through a combination of syndicated loans and private equity investments, with capital markets specialists coordinating the financing.

Real estate developers focused on creating flexible spaces that could accommodate a variety of tenants, from small manufacturers to large logistics companies.

Sustainability was a key consideration, with the industrial park incorporating green building certifications and renewable energy sources.

The project's success highlighted the importance of collaboration between real estate and capital markets.

By aligning financial strategies with market demand, the industrial park became a hub for economic activity and innovation.

Case Study 8: Healthcare Real Estate Fund

A healthcare real estate fund was established to invest in properties such as hospitals, clinics, and senior living facilities.

The fund raised capital through institutional investors, including pension funds and insurance companies, seeking stable returns.

Capital markets played a central role in structuring the fund, ensuring that it met the specific needs of healthcare-focused investors.

Real estate developers partnered with healthcare providers to design properties that prioritized patient care and operational efficiency.

The project demonstrated the resilience of healthcare real estate as an asset class, particularly during periods of economic uncertainty.

By leveraging capital markets expertise, the fund successfully balanced risk and reward, delivering value to both investors and communities.

Case Study 9: Student Housing Portfolio

A student housing portfolio was developed to address the rising demand for affordable accommodations near universities.

Real estate developers collaborated with a real estate investment trust (REIT) to finance the project, leveraging the REIT's access to capital markets.

The portfolio included a mix of dormitories and shared apartments, designed to meet the needs of modern students.

Developers incorporated energy-efficient designs and communal spaces to enhance the living experience, aligning with ESG principles.

The project underscored the potential of specialized real estate funds to address niche market needs.

By integrating real estate and capital markets strategies, the portfolio achieved financial success while supporting educational initiatives.

Case Study 10: Mixed-Use Urban Development

A mixed-use urban development project was launched to create a self-sustaining community with residential, commercial, and recreational components.

The project was funded through a combination of equity crowdfunding and traditional bank loans, ensuring a diverse capital base.

Real estate developers prioritized inclusivity, designing affordable housing units alongside premium apartments and integrating public spaces such as parks and community centers.

Capital markets specialists structured the crowdfunding campaign to attract retail investors, emphasizing the project's social and environmental impact.

The success of the project demonstrated the power of combining real estate innovation with capital markets expertise.

By engaging a broad range of stakeholders, the development became a model for sustainable urban living.

Lessons from the Case Studies

The case studies presented in this chapter illustrate the vast opportunities available at the intersection of real estate and capital markets.

Each case reveals how strategic thinking, innovative approaches, and effective collaboration can lead to successful outcomes, even in the face of complex challenges.

Together, these examples underscore the transformative potential of aligning real estate projects with capital markets expertise, offering lessons that extend beyond individual ventures and resonate across the industry.

One of the most striking lessons is the importance of adaptability. The featured projects showcase how developers and investors have embraced new technologies, market trends, and financial instruments to meet evolving demands.

Whether leveraging blockchain for tokenized residential investments or utilizing green bonds to fund sustainable office towers, these initiatives demonstrate that flexibility and innovation are critical to staying competitive.

Real estate professionals and capital markets specialists must remain open to exploring novel approaches and adopting tools that enhance efficiency, transparency, and inclusivity.

The case studies also highlight the significance of collaboration between sectors.

Real estate projects are inherently multidisciplinary, requiring input from architects, developers, financiers, and policymakers. When these stakeholders work in harmony, as seen in the urban redevelopment and logistics hub projects, the results can create lasting economic, social, and environmental benefits.

For capital markets specialists, engaging with real estate professionals ensures that financial products are tailored to the specific needs of the industry, fostering mutual success.

Another key takeaway is the growing role of sustainability in real estate capital markets. Several of the case studies emphasize the importance of ESG principles, from the green office tower funded through green bonds to the affordable housing REIT prioritizing social equity.

These examples reflect a broader shift in investor priorities, with stakeholders increasingly valuing projects that balance profitability with positive social and environmental impact. This trend presents a significant opportunity for real estate professionals to differentiate their offerings and attract capital by incorporating sustainability into their projects.

For investors, the case studies reveal the potential for diversification within real estate capital markets.

By participating in niche sectors such as healthcare facilities, student housing, or logistics hubs, investors can achieve stable returns while mitigating risks associated with traditional asset classes.

These opportunities highlight the importance of understanding market dynamics and identifying sectors poised for growth, allowing investors to position themselves strategically in an increasingly competitive landscape.

The lessons extend beyond financial strategies to include operational excellence.

Projects like the mixed-use urban development and industrial park expansion illustrate how meticulous planning and attention to detail can enhance project outcomes.

From securing the right tenants to incorporating community-focused design elements, these initiatives demonstrate that operational success is as important as securing funding. Real estate professionals must prioritize quality, sustainability, and stakeholder engagement to maximize the value of their projects.

Equally important is the role of technology in shaping the future of real estate capital markets.

The tokenization project and PropTech-driven student housing portfolio highlight the potential of digital innovation to revolutionize traditional practices. These examples underscore the need for stakeholders to embrace technological advancements and leverage them to streamline processes, reduce costs, and enhance the investor experience.

As the industry continues to evolve, those who adopt a forward-thinking approach will be best positioned to succeed.

The case studies also emphasize the importance of managing risks effectively. Real estate capital markets are inherently complex, with projects exposed to a wide range of economic, regulatory, and operational risks.

By conducting thorough due diligence, employing robust risk management strategies, and collaborating with experienced partners, stakeholders can mitigate these challenges and ensure long-term resilience.

The healthcare real estate fund and cross-border retail investment projects, for instance, demonstrate how careful planning and strategic partnerships can help navigate uncertainties and capitalize on opportunities.

These lessons serve as a call to action for professionals across the real estate and capital markets industries.

For real estate developers, the message is clear: align your projects with market demands, embrace sustainability, and adopt innovative financing models to attract investment and achieve lasting impact.

For capital markets specialists, the case studies highlight the need to understand the intricacies of real estate projects and develop financial products that address their unique requirements.

For investors, the opportunities presented in these case studies underscore the importance of diversification, both in terms of asset classes and geographical markets.

By exploring emerging sectors and leveraging cutting-edge technologies, investors can unlock new avenues for growth and achieve resilient portfolios. The examples also encourage investors to prioritize ESG-aligned projects, recognizing the growing demand for sustainable and socially responsible investments.

The interplay between real estate and capital markets is a dynamic and evolving relationship, offering immense potential for those who are willing to embrace change and think strategically.

The case studies in this chapter provide a blueprint for success, demonstrating how innovative approaches and collaborative efforts can drive value creation across the industry. However, these lessons are only valuable if acted upon.

For those looking to seize the opportunities outlined here, the first step is to engage actively with the broader ecosystem of real estate and capital markets.

Attend industry events, build networks with professionals from complementary sectors, and stay informed about emerging trends and technologies.

By fostering collaboration and knowledge-sharing, you can position yourself to capitalize on the interconnected nature of these industries.

The next step is to integrate sustainability and innovation into your strategies.

Whether through ESG-aligned investments, PropTech adoption, or tokenized assets, embracing these principles will not only enhance your projects but also align them with the priorities of investors, tenants, and communities. By prioritizing long-term value over short-term gains, you can build a foundation for sustainable success in real estate capital markets.

Finally, take inspiration from the case studies and apply their lessons to your own projects and investments.

Every venture is unique, but the underlying principles of adaptability, collaboration, and strategic thinking remain universal.

By approaching challenges with creativity and a willingness to explore new possibilities, you can transform risks into opportunities and achieve remarkable outcomes.

The case studies in this chapter represent a glimpse into what is possible when real estate and capital markets come together.

They highlight the potential for innovation, resilience, and impact, offering a roadmap for navigating the complexities of this interconnected industry.

As we look ahead to the future, the opportunities are boundless for those who are ready to take action and embrace the transformative power of real estate capital markets.

Let's now dive into the last chapter of this book as a conclusion to our journey.

Chapter 16: Conclusion

The journey through the interconnected world of capital markets and real estate has illuminated a dynamic, multifaceted relationship that is reshaping how professionals operate, innovate, and invest.

From understanding the foundational principles to exploring advanced strategies and technologies, this book has provided a comprehensive roadmap for navigating the complexities of these interwoven industries.

As we conclude, it is essential to consolidate the insights from previous chapters, propose actionable strategies, and outline a forward-looking vision for stakeholders in this transformative space.

Let's conclude with a summary of insights, strategies, opportunities and a roadmap for success.

A Summary of Insights

At the heart of this book lies the recognition that capital markets and real estate are no longer distinct entities but parts of a unified ecosystem. The early chapters introduced the foundational concepts, emphasizing the historical evolution of these markets, their unique characteristics, and their growing interdependence. Real estate professionals learned how to view their industry through the lens of financial markets, while capital markets specialists gained insights into the nuances of real estate investments.

The exploration of debt and equity financing highlighted the critical role of funding structures in shaping real estate projects. These chapters underscored how mortgages, bonds, and equity instruments are fundamental tools for aligning capital with opportunity. Readers gained practical knowledge about leveraging these instruments to optimize project outcomes, balance risk, and maximize returns.

Technology emerged as a transformative force throughout the book, particularly in discussions of blockchain, PropTech, and tokenization. These tools are not merely add-ons but catalysts for efficiency, transparency, and accessibility. Their ability to streamline processes and create new investment opportunities reflects the profound impact of innovation on the real estate capital markets landscape.

Sustainability and ESG principles also stood out as critical themes, shaping both investor preferences and development priorities. The integration of environmental, social, and governance factors into real estate strategies aligns with broader societal goals and enhances the long-term value of assets. These insights resonate across all stakeholders, offering a pathway to ethical and impactful investments.

Finally, the case studies provided real-world examples of how capital markets and real estate intersect in practice. From urban revitalization to cross-border investments, these scenarios illustrated the diverse opportunities and challenges that define this evolving relationship. The lessons drawn from these examples serve as a foundation for actionable strategies and forward-thinking approaches.

Strategies for Success

To succeed in the interconnected world of capital markets and real estate, stakeholders must adopt strategies that reflect the insights and lessons from this book.

One of the most critical strategies is to embrace innovation. Technology is not optional; it is a necessity for staying competitive and relevant. From blockchain-enabled transactions to data-driven decision-making, the tools of the future are available today. Stakeholders must invest in these technologies, understand their applications, and leverage them to gain a strategic edge.

Collaboration is another cornerstone of success. Real estate and capital markets professionals cannot operate in silos. Developers must engage with financial experts to structure deals that attract investment, while investors must understand the intricacies of real estate projects to make informed decisions. Partnerships, joint ventures, and cross-sector dialogues are essential for bridging gaps and creating shared value.

Sustainability is no longer a secondary consideration; it is a primary driver of investment decisions and development strategies. ESG principles should be integrated into every stage of the real estate lifecycle, from planning and financing to construction and management. This approach not only aligns with investor preferences but also ensures long-term resilience and relevance in an increasingly sustainability-focused world.

Diversification is a key strategy for mitigating risk and maximizing returns. Real estate professionals should explore opportunities across different asset classes, geographical markets, and emerging sectors. Capital markets specialists, in turn, can benefit from incorporating real estate into their portfolios as a stable and tangible asset class that complements traditional securities.

Education and adaptability are equally important. The rapidly changing landscape of real estate capital markets requires stakeholders to stay informed, continuously update their skills, and adapt to new trends and challenges. Lifelong learning and a willingness to evolve are essential for thriving in this dynamic industry.

Opportunities and a Roadmap for the Future

Looking ahead, the opportunities in real estate capital markets are boundless.

Urbanization, globalization, technological advancements, and shifting societal priorities are creating new avenues for growth and innovation.

By understanding and leveraging these trends, stakeholders can position themselves to capitalize on emerging opportunities while addressing potential challenges.

One of the most promising opportunities lies in the integration of technology. The rise of smart cities, powered by IoT, AI, and blockchain, represents a transformative shift in how urban spaces are designed, developed, and managed.

Real estate professionals and capital markets specialists must collaborate to fund and implement these initiatives, creating smarter, more efficient, and more sustainable communities.

Sustainability will continue to be a driving force, with green buildings, renewable energy projects, and eco-friendly developments gaining traction. These initiatives align with ESG principles and cater to a growing segment of investors and tenants who prioritize environmental and social impact.

By embracing sustainability, stakeholders can differentiate themselves and build lasting value.

Globalization remains a critical theme, with cross-border investments offering opportunities for diversification and growth. However, stakeholders must navigate the complexities of international markets, including regulatory differences, cultural nuances, and currency risks.

By adopting a global perspective and leveraging technology to bridge gaps, real estate capital markets can unlock the potential of international opportunities.

The roadmap for the future also includes a focus on inclusivity and accessibility. Real estate capital markets must prioritize initiatives that address housing affordability, community development, and equitable access to resources.

By aligning financial goals with social impact, stakeholders can create projects that benefit both investors and society at large.

To move forward effectively, stakeholders should focus on building resilience. The challenges of climate change, economic uncertainty, and geopolitical tensions require strategies that anticipate and mitigate risks.

From scenario planning to diversified investments, resilience is the foundation for navigating uncertainty and seizing opportunities.

Closing Thoughts

This book has provided a comprehensive exploration of the interconnected world of capital markets and real estate, offering insights, strategies, and examples to guide stakeholders in this dynamic space. The journey has covered foundational principles, advanced strategies, and real-world applications, culminating in a roadmap for the future.

As we conclude, the message is clear: the convergence of capital markets and real estate is not just a trend; it is a defining feature of the industry's future. The opportunities are vast, the challenges are real, and the potential for impact is profound.

The way forward is not simply to react to change but to shape it. With the knowledge and strategies outlined in this book, readers are equipped to take proactive steps, build meaningful partnerships, and create projects that define the future of real estate capital markets.

The path ahead is one of discovery, innovation, and growth, and the journey begins now.

Author Bio

Willem Tait is an accomplished author, real estate expert, and industry mentor whose journey through the world of property investment and capital markets has inspired professionals across the globe. With decades of experience, Willem has become a trusted voice in real estate strategy, capital markets integration, and the transformative power of mentorship.

Willem's passion for education and professional growth is reflected in the six insightful books authored to date. Each work delves into the intricate dynamics of real estate, offering practical strategies, actionable insights, and thought-provoking perspectives on topics ranging from sustainability and innovation to navigating complex financial landscapes. This prolific body of work solidifies Willem's position as an authority in the field, bridging the gap between theory and practice with clarity and expertise.

Beyond writing, Willem Tait holds a strong academic foundation, having pursued advanced studies that inform a nuanced understanding of real estate, economics, and market trends. This dedication to lifelong learning complements a hands-on approach, mentoring aspiring professionals to achieve their goals in real estate and beyond. Known for his ability to break down complex concepts into accessible knowledge, Willem empowers readers and mentees alike to navigate the evolving challenges of the industry.

Whether guiding readers through the intricacies of capital markets or inspiring the next generation of leaders, Willem Tait continues to shape the conversation around real estate and its future.

This blend of expertise, passion, and a commitment to growth ensures that Willem remains not just a specialist, but a trailblazer in the ever-changing world of real estate and capital markets.

Acknowledgements

This book represents not only my passion for real estate and capital markets but also the invaluable contributions of countless individuals who have supported, guided, and inspired me throughout its creation. I want to express my deepest gratitude to all those who played a part in bringing this vision to life.

To the professionals in the capital markets realm, bankers, funders, and investors, your insights and expertise have been instrumental in helping me understand and articulate the complexities of this fascinating sector. The conversations and consultations we shared provided a wealth of knowledge that has enriched the content of this book, ensuring its relevance and accuracy.

To the incredible minds in the real estate industry, developers, real estate professionals, quantity surveyors, and architects, your dedication to shaping our built environment is nothing short of inspiring. Thank you for sharing your experiences, challenges, and triumphs, which have allowed me to bridge the practical realities of real estate with the dynamic opportunities of capital markets.

This work would not have been possible without the countless individuals who gave their time to engage in interviews, discussions, and brainstorming sessions. Your generosity in sharing your expertise has made this book a truly collaborative effort. While I cannot name everyone here, I hope you know how deeply I appreciate your willingness to contribute to this endeavor.

Finally, to my readers, this book is for you. It is my hope that through the pages of this work, you will see the immense potential that lies at the intersection of real estate and capital markets. The globalization of these industries is a monumental shift, and I am honored to have the opportunity to introduce you to the possibilities it holds.

Thank you to everyone who has been a part of this journey. Your contributions, whether large or small, have been deeply felt and are reflected in every word of this book. This is not just my work; it is ours. Together, we are shaping the future of real estate capital markets.

List of Books to Date

Willem Tait has authored several insightful books that explore the dynamic and evolving relationship between real estate and capital markets. Each book delves into critical aspects of the industry, offering readers actionable strategies, practical insights, and a deeper understanding of the forces shaping the market. Below is the complete list of books to date:

1. Real Estate Law Essentials: Navigate Cross-Sections, Avoid Pitfalls, and Seize Opportunities
   A comprehensive guide to understanding the legal frameworks surrounding real estate, offering practical advice for navigating transactions and mitigating risks.
2. Proven Principles of Residential Real Estate Investment: Strategies and Tasks for Building Generational Wealth
   A detailed exploration of residential real estate investment strategies, designed to help readers achieve long-term financial security and success.
3. Practical Principles of Commercial Real Estate Investment: Tasks and Strategies for Real Estate Success
   Focused on commercial real estate, this book

provides actionable principles and strategies for navigating the complexities of the market and achieving professional growth.
4. Real Estate Economics: Property Market Principles and Practices
This book offers an in-depth analysis of real estate markets, their underlying principles, and the economic forces driving them.
5. Raising Money for Real Estate Investment: Close Deals, Raise Money, Build Wealth
A practical guide to securing funding for real estate projects, this book emphasizes effective deal-making and wealth-building strategies.
6. Capital Markets and Real Estate: Bridging Markets for a Global Future
This current work explores the intersection of real estate and capital markets, highlighting their convergence and the opportunities that globalization presents for industry professionals.

These books are part of the Real Estate Mastery Books, a series designed to equip readers with the tools and knowledge necessary to excel in the fields of real estate and capital markets. This ever-expanding series reflects Willem Tait's commitment to providing actionable insights and strategies.

Keep an eye out for upcoming titles in this growing collection, as there are always more exciting additions to come.

Social Profiles

Willem Tait is committed to staying connected and engaging with his readers. He is active on LinkedIn and X (formerly Twitter), where he shares updates on his latest projects, insights, and resources. Willem is also available for face-to-face consultations, public speaking, and group training sessions through platforms like WhatsApp, Zoom, Google Meet, and Microsoft Teams.

Feel free to reach out on any of these platforms to connect, share ideas, or discuss opportunities for learning and growth. Let's keep building together!

LinkedIn: https://www.linkedin.com/in/willemtait/
X (previously Twitter): https://x.com/willemtait
Calendly: https://calendly.com/willemtait
Email: willemtait@outlook.com

Mentorship, Consulting and Public Speaking

As a dedicated professional with a passion for real estate, business, law, and economics, I thrive on sharing actionable insights and practical strategies that empower individuals and teams to achieve their goals. My expertise spans real estate investment, business consulting, personal growth, and the intricate connections between legal and economic frameworks, allowing me to offer a well-rounded perspective tailored to diverse challenges and ambitions.

Through public speaking engagements, customised mentorship programs, and dynamic one-on-one or group coaching sessions, I aim to inspire, educate, and guide. Whether addressing an audience of hundreds or working closely with a small team, my mission is to deliver value-driven insights that leave a lasting impact.

If you're seeking a keynote speaker to energise and inform your event, a consultant to elevate your business strategies, or a mentor to foster personal and professional growth, I'm here to collaborate. My approach integrates years of hands-on experience with a solid foundation in real estate, law and economics, ensuring the strategies I share are both practical and informed by robust principles.

Let's connect to explore how I can help you or your organisation unlock new opportunities and achieve meaningful success. Together, we can create strategies that inspire growth, drive innovation, and deliver measurable results.

LinkedIn: https://www.linkedin.com/in/willemtait/

Mail: willemtait@outlook.com

I Value Your Feedback

Your thoughts and opinions matter deeply to me. Writing this book has been a journey of exploration and growth, and your feedback plays a vital role in shaping how I approach future works. Whether you've gained new insights, found areas that resonated with your experience, or have suggestions for improvement, I would love to hear from you. Your constructive criticism helps refine my writing and ensures these books continue to provide value to readers like you.

If you enjoyed this book or found it helpful, I encourage you to leave a review. Share what stood out to you, what you learned, and how the content might have impacted your perspective on real estate and capital markets. Your review can guide others in deciding if this book is the right resource for them, while also helping me understand what resonates most with readers.

For those who have suggestions or ideas, I welcome your input. Are there topics you'd like to see explored in future books? Areas where I could provide deeper insights? Your suggestions are invaluable in ensuring this series continues to evolve and meet the needs of a diverse audience.

Thank you for taking the time to share your feedback. Your thoughts, whether through a review or direct suggestions, are a gift that helps me grow as an author and ensures that these books remain a meaningful resource for readers around the world. I look forward to hearing from you.

Willem Tait

Updated Portfolio of Books

For more, kindly see www.amazon.com/author/willemtait

BUSINESS BOOKS

1. **Real Estate Law Essentials:** Navigate Cross-Sections, Avoid Pitfalls, and Seize Opportunities.
2. **Proven Principles of Residential Real Estate Investment:** Strategies and Tasks for Building Generational Wealth.
3. **Practical Principles of Commercial Real Estate Investment:** Tasks and Strategies for Real Estate Success.
4. **Real Estate Economics:** Property Market Principles and Practices.
5. **Raising Money for Real Estate Investment:** Close Deals, Raise Money, Build Wealth.
6. **Capital Markets and Real Estate:** How Money and Capital Shapes the Property Market.
7. **Real Estate Development and Deal Making:** The Essential Guide for Property Developers, Entrepreneurs, and Dealmakers.
8. **Psychology of Residential and Commercial Real Estate:** Master the Psychology Behind Real Estate Success.
9. **Philosophy of Residential and Commercial Real Estate:** Exploring the Intersection of Philosophy, People, Property, Purpose and Spaces.
10. **Economics of Banking and Money:** Insight into Power, Trust, and Change.
11. **The Future of Real Estate:** PropTech, Sustainability and Design

SELF-HELP AND MOTIVATIONAL BOOKS

1. **Sort Your Crap Out:** Own Your Choices, Silence Your Critic. Get Stuff Done
2. **Dammit, Get It Together:** Stop Making Excuses and Start Living the Life You Deserve
3. **Stop Giving a Damn and Start Living:** Cut the Crap. Focus on What Matters. Live Fully
4. **Dammit, It's Your Life:** Own Your Mind, Time, and Choices
5. **Dammit, Stop Being Overwhelmed and Overworked:** Reclaim Your Time, Energy, and Sanity

ANNOTATED AND COMMENTARY

1. **The Way to Wealth** (Annotated): With Motivational Commentary by Willem Tait
2. **The Art Of War:** (Annotated): Proven Modern Strategies for Winning in Business, Leadership, and Life by Willem Tait

www.ingramcontent.com/pod-product-compliance
Lightning Source LLC
Chambersburg PA
CBHW071529220526
45469CB00003B/695